Instant Pot®
Asian
PRESSURE COOKER MEALS

Fast, Fresh & Affordable

Patricia Tanumihardja

TUTTLE Publishing

Tokyo | Rutland, Vermont | Singapore

Contents

Getting the Most from Your Instant Pot®!

My love-hate relationship with pressure cookers dates back to my childhood. My mother always used a stove-top pressure cooker to whip up her signature *sup buntut*, Indonesian Oxtail Stew. And while I loved that dish, I never wanted to be in the kitchen when Mom was cooking it. The pressure cooker whistled deafeningly and the steam valve would shake, rattle and roll like there was no tomorrow. Scarier still, spurts of steam and water droplets would spew out of the valve. Yes, I was terrified of this "monster." These memories have stayed with me. So when Mom gave me a pressure cooker after I got married, it sat on the shelf gathering dust until I gave it away to Goodwill.

In the last few years, a new generation of electric pressure cookers (or rather multifunction cookers!) has come to the market, with Instant Pot® leading the way. Safer and less intimidating, these appliances are easier to use, and offer the user more control. The latest models have self-regulating safety features, including temperature and pressure sensors inside the unit. All you have to do is plug and play. It's no surprise they're winning over fans every day.

An Instant Pot® is excellent for certain dishes, but there are some recipes that are simply better cooked on the stove or in the oven. But that leaves many, many recipes that should be made in a pressure cooker because it does it better, faster or more flavorfully, and/or with less mess and stress. See where I'm going now? Many traditional Asian recipes, especially curries and braises, require long stints on the stove. With the advent of the electric pressure cooker, the time spent cooking is cut down to a mere hour or so. It has allowed me to reclaim my mother's recipes and many others I've deemed too laborious to make anymore.

So why use an Instant Pot® for Asian cooking?

• Pressure cooking allows you to cut down on braising time for traditionally slow-cooked dishes like Chinese "Red Cooked" Pork (page 105) and Braised Korean Short Ribs (page 81). Cheaper and tougher cuts of meats cook till they fall off the bone with a silky, succulent tenderness.

• It allows for one-pot cooking! You can sauté and pressure cook/slow-cook in the same appliance.

• You can cook your protein, vegetables and/or rice at the same time using the pot-in-pot method (page 12).

• Asian dishes often use a combination of meat and vegetables. The meat is cut into thin strips to perfectly time with large-cut vegetables in the pressure cooker. The electric pressure cooker can also be easily paused to add vegetables toward the end of the cooking cycle and quickly brought up to pressure again.

• Legumes and grains don't require soaking. So even if nothing has been soaked, you can still cook Curried Lentils with Dates and Caramelized Onions (page 42) or Sweet Sticky Rice with Fresh Mango (page 124) and get it done fast.

• Curries and spice-infused dishes are quicker to make (Chicken Rendang Curry, page 96, in 45 minutes!?) and the pressure-cooking process deeply infuses the food with flavor.

• Steaming is a breeze in the pressure cooker—no need to monitor the water in the pot or worry about controlling the heat. Plus, my Steamed Fragrant Fish (page 116) has never turned out so silky and tender!

Note that the modern-day appliances are not just pressure cookers but multifunction cookers with options to sauté, slow-cook, steam and even make yogurt. While you can do myriad things in your Instant Pot®, I took a poll among friends and blog readers and the most popular functions are: sauté and pressure cook. So I have focused on these two most commonly used functions for this book.

The recipes in this book are all designed to work either as one-pot meals or standalone dishes that need only be paired with rice or noodles and a vegetable side dish. While most of them make 4 to 6 servings (as part of a multicourse meal), they can be doubled to serve more people or bigger appetites.

For the busy parent or professional who lacks the time and energy to cook, the electric pressure cooker is a life saver. Some recipes take a mere 30 minutes to cook; others may take longer but are hands-off or a far cry from the hours traditionally required.

If you're an Instant Pot® newbie, you will encounter a bit of a learning curve, especially for the technically challenged like me. But once you get over that hump, it's all pretty intuitive. Think of it like washing rice—once you learn how, you never forget.

With that, I say, go forth and pressure cook!

About Your Instant Pot®

If you're an old hand at using your Instant Pot®, feel free to skip this section. If you're a new user, please read on for some crucial information that will help you get the most out of cooking from my book. BUT, this information is not a replacement for reading your handy dandy manual!

There are many brands of electric pressure cookers. Every manufacturer is different, and every model has its own quirks and special functions. It's very important for you to learn about your individual model firsthand from the manufacturer. Please note that I have an Instant Pot® Ultra 6 Quart Multi Cooker. Since the Instant Pot® Duo is also a very popular model, I use both terminology. Please keep in mind that some functions may be different on your model.

Instant Pot® Parts

Most pressure cookers come with the following parts.

Lid with Steam Valve and Pressure Valve

Steam Valve: a knob that allows a pressure cooker to build or release pressure. When pressure cooking, this valve must be in the "Sealing" (locked) position.

Float (pressure) valve: a metal pin that indicates whether the pressure cooker is pressurized or not; it pops up when the cooker has come to pressure and drops when pressure is fully released.

Outer body: the outer shell with the display panel and buttons.

Inner pot: the removable stainless-steel pot where food is cooked. It cleans easily, but food does get stuck on. Instant Pot® sells a ceramic nonstick version.

Steamer rack or trivet: most brands of electric pressure cookers come with a metal stand that's useful for steaming foods.

Condensation collector: a cup used to collect any liquid that condenses while cooking.

Functions

The newer pressure cooker models have a gazillion functions, but I use only two in my cookbook: Sauté and Pressure Cook/Manual. You might find functions like "Soup," "Meat," "Steam" and "Egg," but they all technically use pressure cooking. To make it easier, I use the "Pressure Cook/Manual" function whether I'm braising meat, making rice porridge or simmering soup.

Sauté Function: The Sauté mode on my own pressure cooker has three heat levels that change with a twirl of the dial—LOW, MEDIUM and HIGH. With the Instant Pot® Duo, the heat level is controlled by the "Adjust" button.
• MEDIUM/NORMAL: ~160°C (320°F) for regular browning
• HIGH/MORE: ~170°C (338°F) for darker browning
• LOW/LESS: ~105°C (221°F) for light browning
I tend to use "MEDIUM/NORMAL" for most things, except for browning meats. For boiling, or if I'm in a hurry, I adjust to "HIGH/MORE." In my opinion, the Sauté function isn't as effective for browning as on the stove. It can happen, but it might take a while. So when I'm in a hurry, I'll do this step on the stovetop. Sautéing on the stovetop uses one more pan but helps prevent the "Burn" notice that newer pressure cookers seem to be plagued with. I find this especially helpful when I'm cooking foods that like to stick to the pot, like egg or onions. You can also lessen this problem by buying a ceramic insert, which is pretty much nonstick.

Pressure Cook Function: The "Pressure Cook" function is the reason why most people buy an electric cooker. By cooking food at a lower temperature and at a higher pressure, the food is cooked faster than on the stove or in the oven. With the Instant Pot® Duo, the "Pressure Cook" function is called the "Manual " function. Like a slow cooker, using the "Pressure Cook" function is convenient—you can just dump your food in your Instant Pot® and go do something else. Shortcuts include: dried legumes don't need to be soaked, congee doesn't need to be stirred and searing meats isn't always required. The best part though is that you can get dinner on the table within 30 minutes. There are two options for pressure cooking: High Pressure (12 to 12.5 psi) or Low Pressure (4 psi and 7 psi). Most of my recipes require the High Pressure function, but several with delicate ingredients like seafood, egg and certain vegetables use low pressure. Check the recipe carefully and adjust to the appropriate pressure before setting the time. At 12 psi, the fibers in vegetables and meat break down quickly, allowing foods to be cooked in a short amount of time.

Notes for Pressure Cooking

When the pressure-cooking time ends, the machine will automatically switch to the "Keep Warm" function (unless you change it to "Off"). At this point, you can either manually release the pressure or let the cooker gradually release pressure on its own (natural pressure release).

Manual or Quick Pressure Release: When you manually release the pressure, the cooking process stops quickly and prevents overcooking. It's ideal for delicate foods like noodles, vegetables and seafood.
• Use it when adding ingredients—usually vegetables—to the pot halfway through cooking.
• Don't use it with foods that have a large liquid volume or high starch content (such as congee or soup).
• Don't use it with foods that foam—may clog the float valve.
• Don't use it with ingredients like beans that may break apart with the sudden change in pressure or temperature.
• Don't use it if the recipe calls for Natural Pressure Release. The food may come out undercooked.

When the Instant Pot® has finished cooking and starts to beep, use a wooden spoon or wear heatproof mitts to manually release the pressure by pressing the quick release button, or moving the pressure release knob from "Sealing" to "Venting." Steam will shoot out, so stand back! You might be intimidated the first few times but you'll get used to it. (And remember: don't release pressure with your cooker under or near your kitchen cabinets). Within a few minutes, the pressure will be fully released and the float valve will drop. Press CANCEL. Unlock the lid and lift it off carefully.

Natural Pressure Release: For a Natural Pressure Release, you don't have to do anything. The pressure simply decreases gradually. However, the food continues to cook. So take that into account when determining your cook time. Since the pressure is released gradually, there is less movement in the pressure cooker. Stock and soup come out cleaner, and foods are more likely to stay intact. If a recipe calls for a manual release, you can still release the pressure naturally if you prefer, but reduce the cook time.
• Use when cooking dried beans and legumes, rice, soup and other foods that foam and/or contain lots of liquid.
• Use when cooking large cuts of meat. Just as you'd let a steak or pork chop rest after grilling, a slow natural release allows the meat to relax and become more tender.
 When the pressure cooker is finished cooking and starts to beep, let the pressure release slowly

by leaving the pressure release knob in the "Sealing" position.

When the pressure is fully released, the machine will not beep or signal when this happens. But you can see the dropped float valve and will be able to unlock the lid. Press CANCEL.

A natural pressure release can take anywhere from 10 to 40 minutes. It varies depending on the ingredients and amount of liquid in the pressure cooker.

Hybrid Pressure Release: A hybrid release uses both the natural and manual methods of pressure release. Allow the pressure cooker to release pressure naturally for several minutes and then manually release the remaining pressure. You can do this to save time and reduce the chance of food splattering out from the float valve. It also allows the meat to rest and tenderize a little.

Zero (0) Minute Pressure Cook Time: Yes, there is such a thing as a "Zero" minute cook time! The food starts cooking from the moment the pressure cooker starts to build up pressure (and while it releases pressure). When the time is up, manually release the pressure. Certain foods like cauliflower, shrimp or rice noodles will be fully cooked just as the pot reaches pressure. And this is when the "Zero" minute comes in.

Instant Pot® Accessories

Once you know what you can and want to do with your pressure cooker, you can decide what additional items you might need. Here are the ones I own.

1. Steamer rack

A steamer rack sits in the inner pot and keeps food raised above the liquid. If you bought an Instant Pot®, a short steamer rack (also called a trivet) with handles already comes  with the kit. It's perfectly fine for setting containers on for steaming. However, it's not tall enough for pot-in-pot cooking. I really like the racks that are designed specifically to hold eggs upright during cooking (mine came in a set of two). They ensure that you end up with perfectly centered yolks every time you cook eggs in the pressure cooker. Plus, they're also taller and ideal for pot-in-pot cooking to steam veggies or rice.

2. Sealing rings

I really like having extra sealing rings for the lid. For one thing, I wash my rings in the dishwasher and I don't run it every day. So having extras is convenient. Also, since odors tend to cling to rubber, I use different colors for sweet and savory recipes. This way, you don't end up with curry-flavored flan.

3. Glass lid

If you want to keep your food warm in your Instant Pot®, or like using the slow-cook function, a glass lid allows you to see what's happening inside.

4. Heatproof mitts or gloves

You can use regular oven mitts to remove a hot insert from your

pressure cooker, but mini silicon mitts fit nicely in the tight space between the ridge of the inner pot and the outer shell. Regular oven mitts may be too thick.

5. Wooden spatula
I love my flat-edged wooden spatula for scraping the brown bits from the bottom of the pot without scratching.

6. Soufflé dish or round cake pan
I already own a ceramic soufflé dish and round metal cake pan that measure about 7½ inches (19 cm) in diameter. They are ideal for pot-in-pot cooking in my

6-quart (5⅔-liter) Instant Pot®. You will need different-sized ones for a different pressure cooker. Look through your cupboard first to see if you have a container that fits in your pressure cooker with about a ½-inch (1¼-cm) clearance all around. Provided they are oven-safe, you can use metal, ceramic or silicon containers. They should all work, but cooking times may vary.

7. Spiders and other extra utensils
A spider or strainer is great for scooping out ingredients while leaving the liquid behind. Extra small bowls are also good to have

on hand for prepped ingredients and condiments.

Alternate Accessory: Drop lid (*Otoshibuta*)
A drop lid or *otoshibuta* is an essential part of the Japanese kitchen arsenal. Often made from wood, the round lid is slightly smaller than the diameter of the pan you're using and floats on top of the simmering foods. You can make your own using parchment paper. I've also had success using a food-safe silicon suction lid. It's great for even cooking and for cooking with minimal liquid.

Useful Tips

Mastering how to cook with the Instant Pot® involves a learning curve. I'm happy to share what I know, dispel some myths and help you avoid any pitfalls.

1. Manage your expectations

First and foremost, understand that just because it's called an Instant Pot® doesn't mean the recipes are ready in an instant. Not all pressure cooker recipes are quick. In this cookbook, I've included recipes that require minimal time and effort. I also have recipes that used to take three or four hours on the stove but have been cut to an hour or so. I think that's a huge improvement! Plus, once the cooking starts, you can just walk away and do other stuff.

Not all recipes will work in the pressure cooker. Recipes where the goal is soft, succulent food and recipes that traditionally take hours are good candidates. Don't expect crispy, crunchy or perfectly seared, and you won't be disappointed!

2. Short cuts if you're in a hurry

There are recipes that call for a natural release (see page 8). If you're in a hurry, do a hybrid release instead of a full natural release. Let the pressure release naturally for at least 10 minutes before manually releasing the rest. The only exceptions are congee and soups; wait at least 20 minutes before releasing manually.

Skip browning the meat. Really! While the reason for browning is clear—you'll get a dish with richer, deeper flavor—it's also messy and takes at least 15 extra minutes. There are other ways to boost flavor: spices, caramelizing sugar, aromatics and fish sauce are all excellent ways. Pressure cooking also extracts more flavor from foods because they are cooked twice as fast and the temperature is double the usual (the maillard effect takes place at 250°F).

Plus, as some of the flavors are extracted, they are condensed back into the sauce or soup.

3. Reheat food in your pressure cooker

You can easily reheat heartier meals like stews and braises in your pressure cooker (try 0 to 5 minutes depending on your food). Instant Pot® also sells a lid for the inner pot, and you can store leftovers directly in it.

4. Using liquids

I try not to use too much liquid in my recipes so I don't have to thicken the sauce too much at the end. For a 6-quart Instant Pot®, I use a minimum of ¼ to ½ cup liquid, depending on the ingredients. Some recipes will let you get by with ¼ cup liquid because vegetables and meat release juices too. Using stock instead of water will add an extra layer of flavor to your dish and is highly recommended!

5. Use cornstarch judiciously

There is a tendency to use a lot of cornstarch in pressure cooking. I prefer to use just the right amount of liquid to produce a good amount of sauce. However, this is not always possible and some thickening is required. Be judicious when adding the slurry (cornstarch-water mixture). Pour it into your sauce slowly and stop as soon as the sauce thickens to your liking. You can always add more if the sauce doesn't thicken properly, but you can't easily repair a gluey, overly thickened sauce.

6. Pot-in-pot method

The pot-in-pot method, or PIP for short, is simple. Pour 1 cup (240 ml) water into the pot and nestle a steamer rack inside. Then place a suitable container with the food on top. Lock the lid and cook. Please use heatproof mitts or gloves to remove your container and rack because they will be very hot. I use PIP cooking for several reasons:

· To cook two different foods at the same time—one directly in the inner pot and one on the trivet, for example, Chicken Adobo (page 95). (The rice cooks on the trivet while the chicken cooks below.)
· I prefer to steam delicate foods like fish, flan and glutinous rice in a separate container.
· PIP cooking makes cleanup easy and convenient, especially when I want to use the pressure cooker to cook two or more dishes in succession.

According to Instant Pot®, you can use any container that is labeled "oven-safe" for PIP cooking. This includes metal, silicone, ceramic and glass. Keep in mind that some materials are better heat conductors than others, so you may need to adjust your cooking time depending on the container you use. Be prepared to add cooking time when using silicone containers and ones with higher or thicker sides. With PIP cooking, consider the cooking times for dishes you want to cook together. For example, Curried Lentils with Dates and Caramelized Onions (page 42) takes about 6 minutes and basmati rice takes 3 minutes, both at high pressure. If I put the basmati rice in a silicone container (it takes a little longer) to cook with the lentils, the timing would work pretty well together. I wouldn't cook brown basmati rice along with lentils, which takes about 25 minutes. Note that PIP cooking is not an exact science, so you'll have to experiment a little. If you're a stickler for perfect rice, your options are:
· Manually release the pressure at the optimum cook time for the rice. Take the rice out, then continue cooking the entree as per the directions.
· Cook the rice separately in a rice cooker or on the stovetop.

7. Releasing steam while doing a manual/quick release

When releasing steam, approach the valve from the side. Use heatproof mitts for extra protection, or a wooden spoon or tongs when turning the valve. Or loosely cover the valve with a dish towel before opening it. This prevents the steam from spurting everywhere. But most important of all: keep your hands and face away from the top of the valve.

Don't release pressure under hanging cabinets, which can be damaged by the steam. Place your pressure cooker on a baking sheet on your stovetop. If you have a flat-top stove, place a towel to protect the surface from scratches. Turn on the fan when you're releasing the pressure to suck up all that steam or to drown out that awful hissing sound.

To encourage the pressure to release faster, you can cool down the temperature of your appliance by draping a damp towel on the metal part of the lid.

8. Deglazing and avoiding the BURN warning

If you use the SAUTÉ function before pressure cooking, please deglaze diligently! Deglazing is a fancy word for the process of adding liquid and scraping the bottom of the pot to remove any browned bits. I mention this in my recipes where applicable, but I'm also saying it here for emphasis. Let the pressure cooker cool briefly before adding liquid. If not, some of the liquid will evaporate instantly, possibly leaving insufficient liquid for the entire pressure cooking time.

9. Tips for Converting Recipes

When converting a recipe, always err on the side of undercooking. You can easily cook your food longer, but an over-cooked dish can't be saved.

Converting a 6-quart pressure cooker recipe for a 3- or 8-quart (2¾- or 7½-l) pot. Different-sized pressure

cookers (and different brands) have different wattages, so they each take different times to build up pressure and release it. The 8-quart model will take the longest to build and release pressure because there is more space to fill and empty. While it may take longer for the 8-quart Instant Pot® to come to pressure than the 3 quart or the 6 quart, once it comes up to pressure, total cooking times should be the same. That means you have to adjust for cooking times and the amount of liquid.

Doubling a recipe. The amount of food and liquid affects how long your pressure cooker takes to come up to pressure. When you double the amount of food, it will take more time to build up pressure. However, once your pot reaches the desired pressure, the cooking time is the same because the steam exerts equal pressure on all surfaces of the ingredients inside the pot. I would advise you to try the recipe as is first and pay attention to how long it takes

to come up to pressure. Then, when you double the recipe, note the difference in time taken to come to pressure. You may want to reduce the cooking time because the food begins to cook once the Instant Pot® starts pressurizing. But if it's a long-cooking braise or stew, it won't make much difference.

10. Use a Drop Lid (*Otoshibuta*)

I swear by a drop lid (page 11) for cooking dishes without too much liquid. It's great for noodles and other foods you don't want to be soggy or overly sauced. How does it work?
· Heat is evenly distributed, allowing the ingredients to cook quickly and evenly as they absorb all the delicious flavors. The cooking liquid circulates toward the lid and coats the top of the ingredients without stirring.
· Ingredients don't break apart. The drop lid holds them in place so they don't move around in the liquid and apart during the cooking process.

My Asian Pantry Staples

These are tried-and-true staples that I always have on hand. Thankfully, many sauces and pastes are pretty similar across cultures, so you can just buy one type, instead of having, say, both shoyu (Japanese soy sauce) and Chinese soy sauce. I try to buy these essentials at an Asian market because they're usually cheaper, but all items should be available in the Asian/Ethnic aisle at your neighborhood grocery store; if not, then at a specialty market.

I'm only featuring the items used in this book, so this list is merely a fraction of what's out there. But these basics will keep you well-supplied for all your Asian dishes, whether prepared in a pressure cooker or otherwise.

Chinese cooking wine
Also known as Shaoxing rice wine, this aromatic cooking spirit is made by fermenting glutinous rice. I add it in moderation to marinades, braises and stir fries. Pale dry sherry is a good substitute. If you don't want to stock different types of cooking spirits, you can use it in recipes that call for sake or mirin (just add sugar). Look for a brand that doesn't contain additives.

Coconut milk
Coconut milk is the creamy, sweet liquid pressed from the freshly grated flesh of mature, brown coconuts. Before opening, always shake the can to mix up the richer coconut cream that rises to the top with the thin milk below (unless told not to do so). Buy unsweetened coconut milk. Check labels to make sure it doesn't contain sugar.

Coconut sugar
Coconut sugar, also called coconut palm sugar, is made from the sap of the coconut palm. It is similar to palm sugar, which is made from the sap of a different palm tree. I used to buy palm sugar in disks or cylinders from the Asian market: I'd have to shave off pieces before measuring it. Then I discovered granulated coconut sugar, and now I'm hooked! It's so much easier to use and available at most grocery stores. Light or dark brown sugar may be used as a substitute, but it doesn't carry the same flavor complexity. Brown sugar is sweeter than coconut sugar, so always start off with less and adjust according to taste.

Coriander seeds
There are two types of coriander seeds. The tiny round, tan ones with a lemony taste are most common. As with all spices, they are best when used whole. The green coriander leaf is what we know as cilantro in North America. Store in a tightly sealed jar for up to 6 months.

Cornstarch
Cornstarch or corn flour is derived from the endosperm of corn kernels. It's used to thicken sauces or soups and also creates a nice crust when frying foods. Tapioca starch or arrowroot are typical substitutes.

Cumin
Available ground and as whole seeds, warm and flavorful cumin comes from a plant that belongs to the parsley family. Widely used in South Asian and Asian cooking, it's an important ingredient in Indian garam masala and many spice blends.

Curry paste
Curry paste is a moist blend of ground or pounded herbs and/or spices. **Thai curry pastes** comprise fresh aromatics such as lemongrass, galangal and chilies that are pounded together into a paste. **Red curry paste** may also include red chilies, shallots, coriander roots, shrimp paste and lime leaves. I applaud you if you want to make curry paste at home, it yields the best flavor and you can control what goes into it. But if you don't want to be hunting down a laundry list of ingredients, a store-bought curry paste works well.

Dried black mushrooms

Succulent and smoky, these mushrooms are popular in Japanese, Chinese and Chinese-influenced cooking. They are sold in cellophane packages and should be stored in a cool, dry place. The mushrooms must be rehydrated before use. See page 37 for instructions. Substitute with fresh meaty mushrooms like shiitakes or cremini.

Dried shrimp

These tiny sun-dried shrimp pack a lot of flavor and impart umami to many Asian dishes like soups and stir fries. Together with other dried seafood like salted fish and scallops, dried shrimp is essential in Cantonese XO sauce.

Dumpling wrappers

Dumpling wrappers are usually made with egg and wheat flour and are available fresh and frozen in myriad shapes and thicknesses. They can be fried, boiled, steamed and even baked, taking on different textures: crispy, springy, chewy or soft as clouds. They're available in different thicknesses and in both round and square shapes. I use thin wonton wrappers in this book. **Gyoza wrappers** would work as well. Keep dumpling wrappers in the refrigerator where they will stay fresh for up to a week. Keep them frozen for up to 2 months. Let them come to room temperature before using. While assembling, cover the stack of wrappers with a damp cloth to keep them moist. The wrappers are very delicate and are prone to tearing. So always buy extra!

Ghee

Ghee is made by simmering unsalted butter until all the water has boiled off and the milk solids have settled to the bottom. The top golden layer is then spooned off. Unlike butter, ghee can be stored unrefrigerated in an airtight container.

Gochugaru

Made from hot Korean red peppers, this brilliant, flaming red powder has a sweet, smoky aroma. In some stores, you can find three grades of the powder. Fine ground powder is used for cooking and making gochujang (see the next entry), coarse-ground for making kimchi and crushed flakes for cooking and as a garnish. Store in a tightly covered jar or plastic bag in the refrigerator where it will stay fresh for several months. Most Asian stores carry it, but if you can't find it, make your own blend. I suggest 1 part ground paprika powder, 1 part ground ancho chili powder and ½ part cayenne or generic chili flakes. You'll get a combination of sweet (paprika), smoky (ancho) and spicy hot (cayenne).

Gochujang

Korean red pepper paste is made from fermented soybeans, glutinous rice, red peppers and malt. Read the labels and buy a brand without additives. Store it in the refrigerator once opened, and it will stay fresh for at least one year.

Mirin

Mirin is a pale gold spirit used in Japanese cooking to add subtle sweetness to salad dressings, marinades and stews. Look for *hon-mirin* (true mirin), a naturally brewed elixir containing natural sugars and avoid *aji-mirin* or any bottle labeled "sweet cooking seasoning." Opened bottles of mirin can be left on the shelf. As a substitute, use ¼ cup dry sherry plus 2 teaspoons granulated sugar.

Miso

Miso is a thick, rich paste made from fermenting any of the following: white rice, barley or soybeans. This flavorful paste is very similar to Chinese *doubanjiang* and Singapore *taucheo*—they are all made from fermented beans (soy, broad or lima). I keep a big tub of miso in my fridge and use it in recipes calling for these other pastes. There are various grades, colors and strengths, but the two most common are white miso (*shiro miso*), a mild, sweet miso, and red miso (*aka miso*) which has a higher salt content and an earthier flavor.

Pandan leaves

Pandan leaves, also called screwpine leaves, are considered the vanilla of Southeast Asian cuisine. They are used to enhance the flavor of sweets and cakes. They also add a subtly sweet flavor and aroma to savory dishes like rice and curries. *Pandan* leaves are available frozen at Asian markets and sometimes fresh. You can buy bottles of artificial *pandan* flavoring, but it's not my first choice.

Noodles

An Asian market is your best bet for buying Asian noodles. But some varieties like pad Thai or lo mein noodles are available in the Asian/Ethnic aisles of local grocery stores.

Cellophane noodles Made from mung bean starch (hence also called mung bean threads), these noodles are translucent and have a smooth and slippery texture, making them perfect for soups. Cellophane noodles are commonly sold dried in packages with 8 to 10 bundles, each ranging from 1.3 to 2 ounces (40 to 60 g). Look for a brand that only uses mung beans and water with no additives.

Chinese wheat or egg noodles Chinese wheat or egg noodles come in various widths and diameters and are available fresh or dried. I only use dried noodles in this cookbook. Lo mein is one variety and is available made with or without egg. Pancit Canton is the Filipino adaptation of Chinese noodles. Substitute with Italian pasta.

Rice noodles Also called rice sticks, rice noodles are made with rice and water. If you are gluten-free, make sure the ingredient list doesn't include wheat starch. Rice noodles come in many sizes. Thin *banh pho* noodles are 1/16-inch (1 mm) in width and most often used in soups, especially the popular Vietnamese Chicken Noodle Soup, (page 50). Medium flat noodles or pad Thai noodles are about 1/8 inch (3 mm) wide. They're the most versatile and can be used in soups, stir fries, salads or as a bed for meat or fish. Round rice noodles (*bún*) are used for Vietnamese Meatballs with Rice Noodles (page 54). They bear a very close resemblance to rice vermicelli or mai fun but are thicker.

Sweet potato noodles Korean noodles made with sweet potato starch and water are called *dangmyeon;* they're the building blocks for Korean Glass Noodles (page 68).

Pepper

Although ground white pepper powder is more commonly used in Asia, I use black peppercorns that I grind directly into my cooking. White pepper is just husked black peppercorns, so which one you use is a matter of preference.

Preserved radish

Preserved radish, sometimes labeled salted radish, comes in both salty and sweet versions. Sweet is preferred for pad Thai. However, preserved radish is generally not very easy to come by, so just buy what you can find—sweet or salty, finely chopped, whole or in long strips.

Rice vinegar

I use rice vinegar for pickling, in dressings and dipping sauces, and a few drizzles will punch up any dish with its mellow acidic flavor. In a pinch, cider vinegar is a good substitute. Try not to use white distilled vinegar, it's much sharper. If you must, use less than what the recipe calls for.

Salt

I buy fine sea salt because it is less processed than iodized table salt and has a more complex flavor. Plus, if you make fermented products like kimchi and pickles, the additives in table salt may interfere with the fermentation process and/or cause the brine to become cloudy.

Sambal oelek

Chili paste, or *sambal* in Malay or Indonesian, is a popular condiment in Southeast Asian cuisine. Indonesian *sambal oelek* is my favorite. Named for the grinding or pounding action used to make it in a mortar, it comprises a mixture of fresh chilies, vinegar and salt. This fiery mixture adds powerful flavor that complements almost any dish. Keep *sambal oelek* in your refrigerator, and it will last for a year.

Seaweed

Kombu, the Japanese name for kelp, is a dark green—almost black—seaweed with a sweet, ocean-fresh scent. It is sold dried in ⅛-inch-thick (3-mm) pliable sheets about 10 by 5 inches (25 by 12.5 cm). *Kombu* is used to make Dashi (page 23). Choose sheets that are very dark and wipe them to remove any grit, but don't rub off the white residue. It's safe and incredibly flavorful. Stored in a cool, dark place, *kombu* keeps indefinitely.

Nori, most familiar as the wrapper for sushi rolls, comes in crisp, thin sheets precut for this purpose. It ranges in color from dark green to deep purple. It is not only used to wrap sushi, but also as a garnish for soups. Keep *nori* in a cool, dark place wrapped up in plastic.

Sesame oil

Thick and amber-colored, sesame oil is pressed from toasted sesame seeds. I use it as a seasoning, not a cooking oil (some cooks do), and drizzle it over stir fries and soups and in marinades.

Sesame seeds

Available in both white and black, sesame seeds are best toasted to bring out their nutty flavor. They're available already toasted, but you can easily do it at home too. Toast a few tablespoons at a time in a small dry cast-iron pan or heavy skillet over medium heat. Stir often to ensure they brown evenly. Once the seeds start popping and turn golden brown, they're ready.

Rice

My family and I eat a lot of rice, and I usually buy a 25-pound (11.3-kilogram) bag of fragrant **white jasmine rice** at one go. I sometimes mix it up with **brown jasmine rice**, which I'll buy in smaller 1- or 2-pound (450- to 900-gram) bags or from the bulk bins. Jasmine rice is our multipurpose rice that we eat with just about everything. I also have a small bag of **Japanese-Style sushi rice** on hand. The gummier texture is more suited for making sushi and other Japanese-Style dishes. **Basmati** is a fragrant, nutty-tasting long-grain rice originally cultivated and grown in India and Pakistan. The longer the grain, the better the quality. Look for cloth packaging, labeled with "extra-long grain." **Glutinous rice** is often called sticky rice. It comes in two colors—white and purple. White sticky rice is not to be confused with Japanese (sushi) short-grain rice. Once cooked, white sticky rice turns from opaque to translucent, and clumps together. Whole-grain purple sticky rice has a sweet, nutty taste and is commonly used for making sweets. If you can't find white sticky rice (it's usually available only at Asian markets), use purple.

Sugar

Organic raw cane sugar is my preferred sugar. Ecofriendly and unrefined, it has the full-bodied taste of sugarcane and is much less processed than white sugar.

Sichuan peppercorns

Sichuan peppercorns may resemble black peppercorns, but they're actually berries. They have a spicy, slightly woodsy flavor and leave a numbing sensation on the tongue. Before using, toast them in a skillet and crush them. To preserve their flavor, keep them in an airtight jar in a cool place. Substitute with an intensely flavored peppercorn like Tellicherry.

Soy sauce

Made from fermented roasted soybeans and ground wheat, there are many different varieties. Chinese soy sauce comes in **regular** and **dark** varieties. **Regular soy sauce** is used for seasoning meats and adding flavor to dishes. Don't confuse regular soy sauce with the "lite" version, which has less sodium. **Dark soy sauce** is aged longer and is rich and robust. A touch of molasses gives it a hint of sweetness. It's used to give braises a nice color. **Japanese shoyu** contains more wheat and is darker and less salty as compared to Chinese. Tamari contains little to no wheat and is great for those who are gluten-free.

Star anise

Star anise is an eight-pronged star-shaped pod that imbues braises and soups with an intense licorice flavor and fragrance. Hard and reddish-brown, it is usually sold in plastic bags and should be stored in an airtight jar away from light and heat. Both star anise and aniseed contain the essential oil anethole, and one can be substituted for the other.

much further to soups and stir fries. I always buy "wet" tamarind. You'll find the sticky, coffee-colored pulp pressed into semipliable blocks and packaged in cellophane. The pulp must be soaked in hot water first to form a paste before using. Tamarind concentrate—processed pulp in a jar or round container—is convenient, but the flavor cannot compare. In a cool, dry place, wet tamarind will last almost forever! Substitute with white vinegar if you must.

Sriracha chili sauce

In the United States, sriracha is synonymous with Huy Fong Foods. The California-based company makes the sauce from chili peppers, distilled vinegar, garlic, sugar and salt. Their signature squeeze bottles with the green cap and a rooster on the front are a fixture on tabletops across the country.

Tamarind

Tamarind is a popular souring agent in Southeast Asian cooking and has a more complex flavor than lime or lemon. You probably know it as a key flavoring in Pad Thai (page 72), but its uses extend

Here's how I make tamarind concentrate at home:

Boil 8 ounces (225 ml) of "wet" tamarind (half a package) with 2 cups water in a medium saucepan over medium-high heat for 8 to 10 minutes. Stir with a wooden spoon to release the pulp. Push the mixture through a fine mesh sieve to yield about 1½ cups of juice.

Combine the remaining pulp with 1 cup warm water, stir and repeat to yield about 1 cup runnier juice. Combine the first "pressing" (1½ cups) with the second (1 cup) to make a total of about 2½ cups. Refrigerate in a sealed container (I use a glass jar) for 2 weeks.

Store-bought tamarind concentrate will vary in tartness. If you're in a pinch, boil 1 cup of store-bought tamarind concentrate in a saucepan on the stove over medium-high heat until it's reduced to ⅔ cup and then use it in the recipes in this book.

Tofu

Tofu is a high-protein, low-fat wonder that is made by coagulating fresh soy milk with a calcium compound until it curdles. The curds are then pressed together to form cakes. Tofu comes in a number of varieties ranging from silky-soft and fragile to firm and dense. What you use depends on your cooking method, and your preferred texture. **Firm or extra-firm tofu** can be sliced, diced and cubed and is sturdy enough for stir fries and deep-frying. Extra firm is drier and less silky, and stands up to pressure cooking.

Delicate silken tofu is only suitable for soups, braises and desserts. Don't try to fry silken tofu—especially not deep-fry—as it can react dangerously with hot oil.

Tofu sheets (yuba, bean curd skin or bean curd sheet) is the film or skin that forms on the surface when soybean

milk is boiled to make tofu. The film is collected and dried into yellowish sheets known as tofu skin. Look for them in cellophane bags in the dried goods section of Asian markets.

Turmeric

Turmeric imbues dishes with a peppery, musky flavor. The fresh rhizome has a rich orange tint and a gingery taste lacking in the ground powdered form. However, the recipes in this book call for only the ground powdered version. Look for turmeric powder that is a pure, deep yellow or gold. Store in an airtight container.

Vegetable oil

With their neutral flavor and high smoke points, vegetable oils (corn, peanut, safflower, soybean, sunflower) are the best choices for Asian cooking. I've been using organic cold-pressed sunflower oil. Feel free to use your choice of oil, but note that different oils add slightly different flavors to your dishes, so it's best to experiment with a variety of oils for different purposes.

Dried chilies

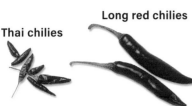

Long red chilies

Thai chilies

Chilies and fresh herbs

Chilies are a very important component of Asian cooking, adding both perfume and heat. Try to obtain a good balance betwen the two when picking chilies, remembering that size and color are not good indicators of their potency. In all the recipes in this book, the amount of chilies you use is up to your discretion. The seeds are the most potent part of the chili, so remove them as needed. One caveat: don't add so much chili that you cannot taste the sweet, salty or sour flavors that make up a dish.

Dried chilies abound, but the small dried red chilies used in Asian cooking tend to be arbol or Japanese chilies. Both are spicy and no longer than 3 to 4 inches (7.5 to 10 cm). Use them whole or ground, roasted or crushed, with or without their seeds. Store them in an airtight container in a cool, dark place.

Long red chilies can be found in an assortment of sizes ranging from 4 to 8 inches (10 to 20 cm) long. The only way to gauge their flavor is to try them. At the grocery store, you might find Fresno (sometimes called red jalapenos), cayenne or Anaheim chilies, and all are good choices. Use only the red, ripe peppers, not the immature green ones. Store them in a closed paper bag in the refrigerator for up to 2 weeks or in plastic in the freezer for 3 months.

Thai chilies or bird chilies are only 1½ inches (4 cm) long, but these fiery little specimens pack a lot of heat into their little bodies. Extremely spicy, they can be used both fresh and dried and come in red, green and sometimes orange. When the green immature chilies ripen, they turn red. Refrigerate in a paper bag for up to 2 weeks or freeze

them fresh, and they should keep well for up to 3 months. Substitute with arbol or serrano chilies if unavailable.

Cilantro/Coriander leaves

Cilantro, or coriander leaf, is used to flavor marinades and also added to noodles, soups and stir fries right before serving as a garnish. The flavorful, earthy-tasting stems and roots are minced and thrown into curry pastes and stocks. Look for whole cilantro/coriander plants with roots at farmers markets or grow your own.

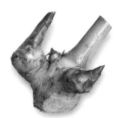

Galangal

Galangal has an earthy aroma and a pinelike flavor with a faint hint of citrus (and is somewhat medicinal). As one of Southeast Asia's most popular aromatics, it's tossed into curries, soups and stews as well as sambals and sauces. Be sure to remove it before serving, as galangal has a hard, chewy texture. Wrap the roots well and they'll stay fresh in the refrigerator for up to three weeks. Or freeze for up to 6 months. Although it is available dried or ground (not a bad idea if you use it sparingly), the fresh form naturally has lots more flavor. Many recipes substitute with ginger. I don't because I think the flavors are oceans apart.

Ginger

Perhaps one of the most versatile and widely used ingredients in Asian cooking, fresh ginger has a warm, zesty flavor and fragrance that add a spicy bite to both sweet and savory dishes. It is used smashed, grated, sliced, chopped,

shredded and juiced. Look for wrinkle-free rhizomes that are firm and with glossy tan skin. Wrap ginger in paper towels, cover with a plastic bag and refrigerate. In my recipes, "chubby" refers to fresh ginger pieces that are about 1 inch (2.5 cm) in diameter.

Lemongrass

These yellowish-green stalks have stiff, lancelike leaves and imbue soups, curries and stir fries with a delicate, citrus flavor. Choose plump stalks that are firm and tight with no signs of mildew or rot. Store fresh lemongrass wrapped in moist paper towels in the refrigerator for up to 2 weeks. Or freeze it in a ziptop bag for 3 months. Lemongrass is available dried (at many spice shops), minced (in the freezer section of Asian markets) and as a paste (in the refrigerated produce section of mainstream grocery stores), but ultimately fresh tastes the best.

Lime leaves, Asian

These glossy, forest-green leaves (previously known as kaffir lime leaves) are wonderfully aromatic. They are also known by their Thai name, *makrut*. Crumble them before adding them to coconut milk dishes, soups and braises for a citrusy, floral undertone. The double-barrel leaves are unmistakable and are best when fresh or frozen. Don't buy them dried if you can help it, as they lack aroma and flavor. Asian lime leaves keep for 10 days in the refrigerator and up to 6 months in a zip-top bag in the freezer. If you can't find them, try substituting lime zest, lemon thyme, lemon verbena or lemon myrtle.

Thai basil

Thai basil's leaves are smaller and more pointed than Italian sweet basil. The burgundy stems are also a dead giveaway. Its flavor, much like licorice, is distinctive in curries and stir fries. Substitute with a mix of Italian basil and mint.

The Basics

From cooking rice to making stock, here are some basics to get you started with your Instant Pot®.

Cooking Rice in an Instant Pot®

The steps for cooking all types of rice are pretty much the same. The table on page 21 lists the approximate times for cooking the different types of rice used in my book. Regardless of rice type, rinse in several changes of water until the water runs clear. I was taught to soak Japanese rice for at least 30 minutes so that moisture penetrates each grain. This ensures the rice grains cook evenly and thoroughly without getting mushy or leaving a hard, uncooked center. In the Instant Pot®, there's really no danger of this so skip this step if you're in a hurry. However, increase the cooking time by a few minutes.

All rice types require a 1:1 ratio of rice to water, even brown rice. Brown rice just needs a longer cooking time for the moisture to penetrate the hull, the tough outer shell.

Whether white or brown, short-grain rice may take a little longer than long-grain rice. Ultimately, the goal is to stop cooking when the rice has absorbed all the water. When you open the lid, give the rice a stir. If there's still unabsorbed water in the pot, cook for a little longer.

Remember these are just guidelines, and you may have to adjust cooking times and ratios to get rice cooked to your liking.

> **NOTES:** To time your rice with other dishes you're making, account for the time it takes for the pressure cooker to build pressure (6 to 10 minutes), and the time it takes for the pressure to release naturally (11 to 18 minutes).
>
> To avoid rice sticking to the bottom of the pot, allow the pressure to release naturally. If you're in a hurry, quick release the pressure after at least 10 minutes of natural release.
>
> I recommend cooking a minimum of 1 cup (200 g) of dry rice directly in the inner pot. If you're cooking less, use the pot-in-pot method (page 12).

PREP TIME: 2 minutes **TOTAL TIME:** 10 minutes
MAKES: 4 servings

1 cup (195 g) jasmine rice
1 cup (240 ml) water

1 Rinse the rice in 2 to 3 changes of water until the water runs clear. Drain in a fine-mesh sieve over the sink. This way, all the water drains from the rice, and you'll use the exact amount of water required.
2 To use the PIP method, pour 1 cup (240 ml) water into the inner pot. Nestle a steam rack inside the pot. Tip the rice into a heat-proof container and place on top of the rack. Pour 1 cup water over the rice.
3 To cook directly in the inner pot, tip the rice in and pour 1 cup (240 ml) water over.
4 Lock the lid. Select PRESSURE COOK/MANUAL and set the pressure to HIGH for 2 minutes. Make sure the steam release valve is sealed. Once pressurized (6 to 10 minutes), the cook cycle will start. When the timer beeps, let the pressure release naturally for 10 minutes. Then quick release any remaining pressure. When the float valve drops, press CANCEL and open the lid.
5 Fluff with a fork and serve.

Cooking Times for Different Types of Rice

Rice	Soak	Rice to Water Ratio	High-Pressure Cook Time
Jasmine (medium- to long-grain) white	No	1:1	3 minutes
Basmati (long-grain) white	No	1:1	3 minutes
Japanese-Style (short-grain) white	Yes: 30 minutes	1:1	3 to 4 minutes
Japanese-Style (short-grain) brown	Yes: 30 minutes	1:1	20 to 24 minutes
Basmati (long-grain) brown	No	1:1	22 minutes

Making Asian-Style Chicken Stock

I like making my own chicken stock. It's cheap, easy and you can control sodium levels. Now, the pressure cooker makes it even easier and faster. To make collagen-rich bone broth, increase your cooking time to 120 minutes. I don't usually add vegetables to my stock, but feel free to do so if you have some on hand.

PREP TIME: 5 minutes **TOTAL TIME:** 70 minutes
MAKES: 8 to 10 cups (2.4 l) stock

1½ to 2 pounds (1 kg) chicken bones (necks, backs and wings are great)
4 medium garlic cloves, peeled and smashed
1-inch (2.5-cm) knob fresh ginger, peeled and cut into coins
2 green onions, chopped into thirds
1 small bunch cilantro/coriander leaves, tied with kitchen twine
1 to 2 cups chopped vegetables (carrots, daikon, celery, onions, leeks, optional)
Water

1 Rinse the bones under cold running water to remove any traces of blood. This process will help produce a clearer stock.

2 Place the bones, garlic, ginger, green onions, cilantro/coriander leaves and vegetables (if using) in the pot. Pour in enough water to cover by 1 inch (2.5 cm), or until the max line is reached.

3 Lock the lid. Select PRESSURE COOK/MANUAL and set to HIGH for 45 minutes. Make sure the steam release valve is sealed. Once pressurized (20 to 30 minutes), the cook cycle will start. When the timer beeps, manually release the pressure. When the float valve drops, press CANCEL and open the lid.

4 Strain the stock through a fine-mesh strainer. Discard the solids. Cool and store in the fridge for 7 days, or freeze for up to 3 months.

> **NOTES:** Instead of chopped vegetables, you can also collect vegetable scraps (peels, stray garlic cloves, onion peels or mushroom stems).
>   If you don't collect bones like I do, use a whole chicken (don't wash the chicken) or 3 to 4 pounds (1.4 to 1.8 kg) cut-up chicken pieces and cook for 20 minutes instead of 45. The shorter cooking time ensures the chicken meat won't be overcooked. Remove the chicken, strain the liquid and use chicken meat and chicken stock as desired.

Making Japanese-Style Dashi Fish Stock

Dashi is the cornerstone of many Japanese dishes, from soups like miso and udon noodle soup to braised dishes. It is easy to make, and my method gives you the option to keep it vegan using only *kombu* (Japanese kelp) or adding dried bonito flakes (*katsuoboshi*) made from skipjack tuna.

PREP TIME: 2 minutes
TOTAL TIME: 7 minutes plus soaking time
MAKES: 3½ cups dashi

6-inch (15-cm) square piece *kombu*, cleaned with a damp cloth
4 cups (960 ml) cold water
1 cup (12 g) dried bonito flakes (optional)

1   Soak the *kombu* in cold water in a medium saucepan for 15 minutes. Place on the stove and heat on medium-high. As bubbles start to appear, discard the *kombu* immediately (or it will become bitter) and remove the pan from the heat. Watch carefully, you don't want the liquid to boil.

2   If using bonito flakes, add ¼ cup (60 ml) water to stop the stock from boiling and immediately add the flakes. Gently swirl the saucepan and strain through a cheesecloth or paper towel into a container. Discard the *kombu* and bonito flakes, or reserve to make a second, weaker batch of dashi. Dashi can be stored in the refrigerator for up to 1 week.

> **NOTES:** *Kombu* and bonito flakes are available in cellophane packaging at Asian markets and some specialty stores.
>
> For a hands-off *kombu*-only dashi, soak it in the water overnight in the refrigerator. This releases most of the flavor without concentrating it. The dashi is ready to use.
>
> *Hondashi* is instant dashi. It contains flavor enhancers like MSG, as well as salt, sugar, yeast extract and dried bonito powder and extract. You can use it in place of from-scratch dashi but adjust the amount of sodium in the recipe.

Soups, Starters & Sides

From quick pickles and cucumber kimchi to soups that can feed a crowd or star in a simple lunch, these starters can kick off the perfect meal.

Homemade Wonton Soup

The wontons I grew up on are a combo of pork, shrimp and/or mushrooms. But feel free to omit any of the ingredients. And just like the street vendors I bought them from, I prefer to poach my wontons in the liquid instead of steaming them. I like to use thinner round Hong Kong-Style dumpling wrappers (they're yellowish in color) or square wonton wrappers.

PREP TIME: 15 minutes **TOTAL TIME:** 25 minutes
MAKES: 4 first-course servings

FILLING
3 ounces (85 g) ground pork
3 ounces (85 g) peeled shrimp, finely chopped
2 tablespoons finely chopped black mushrooms (2 small rehydrated, page 37)
1 tablespoon finely chopped green onions, plus more for garnish
1 teaspoon sesame oil
1 teaspoon Chinese cooking wine
½ teaspoon soy sauce
½ teaspoon grated fresh ginger
½ teaspoon fine sea salt, plus more as needed
Pinch of sugar, plus more as needed
12 round (or square) wonton wrappers, plus more just in case
3 cups (720 ml) low-sodium chicken stock

SPECIAL EQUIPMENT
Steamer rack
Parchment-lined plate
Bowl of water
Damp tea towel

1 Mix together the pork, shrimp, mushrooms, green onions, sesame oil, cooking wine, soy sauce, ginger, salt and sugar in a medium mixing bowl.

2 Arrange your work station: Fill a small bowl with water, cover your stack of wrappers with a damp tea towel and line a large plate with parchment.

3 Scoop 1 tablespoon of filling onto a wrapper. Wet the edge, fold into a half-moon or triangle (depending on the wrapper shape), and gather into a pouch. Set on the prepared plate. Repeat until you have 12 wontons.

4 Pour 3 cups of stock into your Instant Pot®. Gently place the wontons in the stock. Don't worry if the wontons are not entirely submerged.

5 Lock the lid. Select PRESSURE COOK/MANUAL and set to LOW for 0 minutes. Make sure the steam release valve is sealed. Once pressurized (10 to 12 minutes), the cook cycle will start. When the timer beeps, manually release the pressure. When the float valve drops, press CANCEL and open the lid.

6 Scoop up the wontons with a spider or slotted spoon and divide among 4 soup bowls. Season the stock with salt and sugar to taste and pour ½ to ¾ cup (180ml) of stock into each bowl. Sprinkle with green onions and serve immediately.

> **NOTES:** To turn this into a meal for 2 or for small appetites, serve with noodles. Feel free to add more broth after the wontons are cooked.

HOW TO WRAP WONTONS

Japanese-Style Soy Sauce Eggs Ajitsuke Tamago

Japanese-Style soy sauce eggs are delicious served with a big bowl of ramen. But I also love them as a snack or with rice. If you're making Japanese-Style Braised Pork Belly (page 106) you can use the braising liquid to fully submerge the eggs (about 1½ to 2 cups). If not, I provide a marinade for you.

PREP TIME: 1 minute **TOTAL TIME:** 15 minutes plus marinating time

6 large eggs

MARINADE
½ cup (125 ml) water
¼ cup (60 ml) soy sauce
¼ cup (60 ml) sake, Chinese cooking wine or vermouth
¼ cup (60 ml) mirin
2 tablespoons sugar

SPECIAL EQUIPMENT
Steamer rack
Bowl of ice water

1 Pour 1 cup (240 ml) water into the pot and nestle a steamer rack inside. Place the eggs in the middle of the rack.

2 Lock the lid. Select PRESSURE COOK/ MANUAL and set to LOW for 3 minutes. Make sure the steam release valve is sealed. Once pressurized (8 to 10 minutes), the cook cycle will start.

3 Make the marinade while the eggs are cooking. Mix together the water, soy sauce, sake, mirin and sugar in a container that can fit the eggs.

4 Prepare a bowl of ice water.

5 When the timer beeps, manually release the pressure. When the float valve drops, press CANCEL and open the lid.

6 Remove the eggs and immerse in the ice water. Peel the eggs when they have cooled down. Submerge the eggs in the marinade and soak a paper towel on top so they stay submerged. Refrigerate for at least 4 hours or preferably overnight.

> **NOTES:** This recipe makes soft-cooked eggs with a creamy yolk. If you prefer your eggs hard-cooked, cook them at LOW PRESSURE for 8 to 9 minutes.

Seasoned Bamboo Shoots Menma

Seasoned bamboo shoots are also delicious in ramen and as a snack. If you don't have *chashu* braising liquid, you can use the same marinade as the Japanese-Style Soy Sauce Eggs (page 28).

PREP TIME: 1 minute **COOK TIME:** 30 minutes
TOTAL TIME: 31 minutes **MAKES:** ½ cup menma

½ cup (60 g) sliced bamboo shoots, rinsed (fresh, or from a can or package)
1½ cups (350 ml) braising liquid (page 106)
¼ cup (60 ml) mirin
Handful of bonito flakes (optional)

1 Combine the bamboo shoots, *chashu* braising liquid and mirin in a medium saucepan. Add water as needed to cover the bamboo. Bring to a boil over medium-high heat and add the bonito flakes if using. Reduce the heat and simmer for 30 minutes.
2 Remove from the heat and let cool. Transfer the *menma* and marinade into an airtight container and refrigerate overnight. Store in the refrigerator for up to one week.

Pickled Chinese Mustard Cabbage

Chinese mustard cabbage is called *gai choy* in Cantonese, and it's delicious in soups and stir fries. But I like it best of all pickled!

TOTAL TIME: 5 minutes MAKES: 1 quart pickles

BRINE
½ cup (140 ml) hot water
½ cup (140 ml) white vinegar
½ cup (100 g) granulated sugar
2 teaspoons fine sea salt

2 pounds (500 g) mustard cabbage, cut into bite-sized pieces
2 to 3 slices of fresh, peeled ginger

1 Boil a large kettle of water.

2 Make the brine. Stir together the hot water, vinegar, sugar and salt in a large measuring cup. Stir briskly to dissolve the sugar and salt. Set aside to cool.

3 Place the cabbage in a large heatproof bowl and pour just-boiled water over it. Gently stir until the cabbage turns bright green and glistens, 2 to 3 minutes. Drain.

4 Pack the cabbage into a large resealable jar or bottle (at least 1 quart). Tuck in the ginger.

5 Pour the cooled brine over the cabbage, pushing down on the greens to immerse in liquid. Seal and refrigerate 3 to 5 days before eating.

Quick Cucumber Kimchi

Kimchi is a traditional Korean salted and fermented dish made from different vegetables (Chinese cabbage is the most popular) and seasonings. This quick kimchi uses cucumber and not-so-traditional Thai chili.

TOTAL TIME: 10 minutes **MAKES:** 2 cups pickles

SAUCE
2 teaspoons minced garlic (2 cloves)
2 teaspoons grated fresh ginger
2 tablespoons rice vinegar
2 teaspoons fish sauce
2 teaspoons sugar
1 teaspoon gochugaru
2 tablespoons finely chopped green
   onions

8 ounces (225 g) Persian cucumbers or
   other small cucumbers (about 3 or 4)
Toasted sesame seeds, to garnish

1 Mix together the garlic, ginger, vinegar, fish sauce, sugar, gochugaru and green onions in a medium nonreactive bowl.

2 Halve the cucumbers lengthwise. Then cut crosswise into 2 to 3-inch pieces. Mix with the kimchi sauce. Cover and refrigerate for 12 to 24 hours before serving. Sprinkle with sesame seeds. The pickles will keep in the refrigerator for up to 1 week.

> **NOTES:** When cooking with acidic foods, such as vinegar in this case, you need to use a nonreactive container—stainless-steel, enamel-coated or glass—so that food doesn't react with it.

Japanese Savory Egg Custard Chawanmushi

Delicate and silky smooth, this savory Japanese egg custard is usually made with seasonal ingredients. Feel free to use whatever you have on hand, including chicken and/or slices of imitation crab (*surimi*).

PREP TIME: 10 minutes **TOTAL TIME:** 27 minutes
MAKES: 4 (6-ounce) appetizer servings

EGG CUSTARD
2 large eggs
1¼ cups (300 ml) Dashi (page 23), or low-sodium chicken stock
½ teaspoon mirin
½ teaspoon soy sauce
¼ teaspoon fine sea salt
¼ cup carrot sliced on the diagonal about ⅛-inch-thick (3-mm)
2 black mushrooms, rehydrated (page 37) and sliced [2 ounces (60 g)]

TO FINISH
Soy sauce, for drizzling
Chopped green onions, for garnish

SPECIAL EQUIPMENT
Steamer rack
4 (6-ounce) ceramic or glass ramekins
Foil

> **NOTE:** You can use instant dashi powder but taste it before adding soy sauce and salt.
>
> Standard Pyrex ramekins are 6 ounces (180 g). If you don't have ramekins, use heatproof bowls or teacups of similar size.

1 Whisk together the eggs, dashi, mirin, soy sauce and salt in a large bowl.

2 Pour the custard through a fine-mesh sieve into a liquid measuring cup.

3 Divide the carrot and mushrooms among the 4 ramekins. Distribute the custard evenly. Cover each ramekin with foil.

4 Pour 1 cup water into the pot and nestle a steamer rack inside. Place the ramekins on the rack. If they don't fit in one layer, stack them.

5 Lock the lid. Select PRESSURE COOK/MANUAL and set to LOW for 0 minutes. Make sure the steam release valve is sealed. Once pressurized (7 to 10 minutes), the cook cycle will start. When the timer beeps, let the pressure release naturally for 10 minutes. Then quick release any remaining pressure. When the float valve drops, press CANCEL and open the lid.

6 Use heatproof mitts to take out one of the ramekins. Remove the foil and insert a skewer to test for doneness. If the custard looks set and no liquid oozes out, the *chawanmushi* is fully cooked. If not, lock on the lid again and repeat for 0 minutes. When the timer beeps, release the pressure manually for a quick release. The pot will take a shorter time to pressurize.

7 Drizzle with soy sauce to taste and sprinkle with green onions. Serve immediately.

Thai Chicken Coconut Soup
Tom Kha Gai

This Thai soup has such complex flavors that it belies how simple it is to prepare. Your hardest task will be hunting down the ingredients, especially galangal. But trust me, it's worth the effort! Add a bowl of rice to make a meal out of it, and/or serve with other Thai dishes.

PREP TIME: 10 minutes TOTAL TIME: 30 minutes
MAKES: 4 first-course servings

- 6 ounces (170 g) boneless, skinless chicken breast or thighs, sliced into bite-sized pieces
- ½ cup fresh mushrooms like oyster or shiitakes, sliced (2 ounces/60 g)
- 2 cups (480 ml) low-sodium chicken stock
- ¼ cup (60 ml) fish sauce
- 1 teaspoon coconut palm sugar or ½ teaspoon brown sugar
- 6 thin slices fresh galangal
- 3 fresh Asian lime leaves, torn in half and crushed to release essential oils
- 1 plump stalk lemongrass, prepped (page 58), bruised and cut into 3 segments
- 3 to 6 green and/or red Thai chilies, crushed with the butt of a knife (remove the seeds if you don't like it too spicy)
- 1 (13½-ounce/400-ml) can coconut milk
- ¼ cup (60 ml) fresh lime juice (1 large lime)
- Handful cilantro/coriander leaves

1   Mix together the chicken, mushrooms, chicken stock, fish sauce, sugar, galangal, lime leaves, lemongrass and chilies in your Instant Pot®.
2   Lock the lid. Select PRESSURE COOK/MANUAL and set to HIGH for 5 minutes. Make sure the steam release valve is sealed. Once pressurized (6 to 9 minutes), the cook cycle will start. When the timer beeps, let the pressure release naturally for 5 minutes. Then quick release any remaining pressure. When the float valve drops, press CANCEL and open the lid.
3   Stir in the coconut milk and lime juice and mix well. Taste and adjust seasonings if necessary. Fish out the herbs and ladle the soup into individual bowls. Garnish with cilantro/coriander leaves and float 1 chili from the pot in each bowl.

> **NOTE:** If you can't find fresh lime leaves or galangal, frozen or dried versions are fine.
> If frozen, just add them to the soup straight from the freezer.
> If dried, soak them in a bowl of warm water for 10 to 15 minutes, and drain before using.
> And if you do find the fresh herbs, buy in bulk and freeze for later use. They freeze very well.

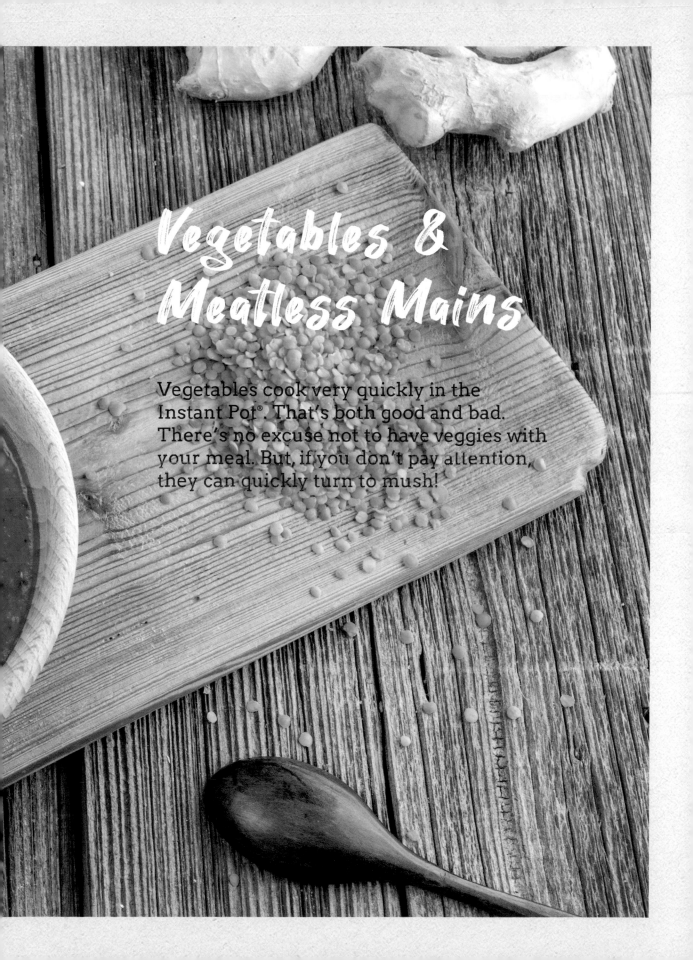

Vegetables & Meatless Mains

Vegetables cook very quickly in the Instant Pot®. That's both good and bad. There's no excuse not to have veggies with your meal. But, if you don't pay attention, they can quickly turn to mush!

Tips for Cooking Instant Pot® Vegetables

Pressure cooking vegetables can be tricky as the intense heat and pressure turn most vegetables to mush in a matter of minutes. You are essentially giving your vegetables a steam bath. You can either cook vegetables on their own in the pressure cooker or cook them with your entree. I give you tips for doing it both ways.

Cooking Vegetables by Themselves

This is a quick way to put a side of vegetables on the table together with a main dish and rice or noodles. I've used cauliflower as an example.

PREP TIME: 2 minutes TOTAL TIME 9 minutes

1 medium head cauliflower
1 cup (240 ml) water

SPECIAL EQUIPMENT
Steamer basket

> **NOTES:** The weight of vegetables and amount of water (although 1 cup is fine for any amount of vegetables) you use will affect the overall results (as these factors affect how long your Instant Pot® takes to come up to pressure). So there's no "one size fits all" magical cooking time.

1 Cut your cauliflower into large, equal florets about 1½ inches (3.75 cm) in size. Arrange the florets in your steamer basket.

2 Pour 1 cup water into the pot and nestle a steamer rack inside.

3 Lock the lid. Select PRESSURE COOK/MANUAL and set to LOW for 0 minutes. Make sure the steam release valve is sealed. Once pressurized (7 to 8 minutes), the cook cycle will start. When the timer beeps, manually release the pressure. When the float valve drops, press CANCEL and open the lid.

4 Rinse the cauliflower under cold running water or place it in an ice bath to stop the cooking. Season with salt, pepper and enjoy.

Vegetable Cooking Table

Vegetable	Shape	Pressure Time
Broccoli (1 medium)	Florets	Low 0
Cauliflower (1 medium)	Florets	Low 0
Green beans (1 pound)	Trimmed	High 0
Carrots (3 medium)	1-inch pieces	High 1 to 2 minutes

Cooking Vegetables with Meat

Often, it makes sense to cook the vegetables and protein together in one pot. Some vegetables are quick-cooking and can be added after the meat is done pressure cooking. Other vegetables are sturdier and can be added at the beginning or halfway through cooking. Here are some tips:

1 Before you start cooking, decide if you're O.K. with slightly mushy vegetables or if you really want them crisp-tender.

2 If you can, cut the meat as thin as possible and the vegetables as thick and large as possible so that cooking times line up.

3 Add the vegetables when the meat is done cooking, and cook on Sauté mode for 2 to 5 minutes. Quick-cooking vegetables like peas, spinach, snow peas and corn work really well. For vegetables like carrots and radishes, cut into strips or slice thinly on the bias for more surface cooking area.

4 For stews, use chunky root vegetables like carrots and potatoes and cut them into large pieces (1½ to 2 inches/3.75 to 5 cm). You can also add them halfway through the cooking process: Manually release the pressure (page 8), add the vegetables and start pressure cooking again where you left off. The pressure won't take as long to build up as the food and appliance are already hot.

5 If you want to "dump and cook," you just might have to be content with slightly mushy vegetables!

HOW TO PREPARE DRIED MUSHROOMS

Rinse then soak the mushrooms in warm water for at least 30 minutes. If you can plan ahead, soak them for 8 hours or more. When the caps are tender, pluck them out and squeeze out the excess water with your hands. Save the soaking water to use in your recipe.

Panang Vegetable Curry with Tofu

Panang is a rich, thick curry that usually has slivers of meat with perhaps some bell pepper strips. My version is different in two ways—I've made it vegetarian and I'm using a semi-homemade curry paste. I simply doctor store-bought red curry paste with distinctive ingredients— peanuts, cumin and lime leaves. This makes the curry truly yummy!

PREP TIME: 10 minutes **TOTAL TIME:** 30 minutes
MAKES: 4 servings

1 can (13½-ounce/400-ml) coconut milk (unshaken)

3 to 4 tablespoons red curry paste (depending on how spicy you like it)

2 to 3 tablespoons peanut butter

1 teaspoon ground coriander

½ teaspoon ground cumin

5 Asian lime leaves, torn in half and crushed, plus 2 leaves sliced thinly for garnish

1 teaspoon fish or soy sauce

1 tablespoon coconut sugar, or 2 teaspoons brown sugar

1 cup cabbage chopped into 2-inch (5-cm) squares (90 g)

1 cup sliced fresh mushrooms like cremini, oyster or shiitake (90 g)

1 package (14-ounce/420-g) extra-firm tofu, patted dry with paper towels and sliced into small cubes

1 cup green beans segments (150 g)

1 cup bell pepper cut into thin strips (90 g)

1 Do not shake the coconut milk can. Scoop out the thick cream on top into a small bowl, leaving the thin coconut milk at the bottom of the can.

2 Select SAUTÉ and set to MEDIUM/NORMAL. Add ¼ cup (60 ml) coconut cream. When the pot is hot, add the curry paste, peanut butter, coriander and cumin and stir and cook until the paste turns a few shades darker and the oil starts to separate, 3 to 4 minutes. Press CANCEL.

3 Stir in ½ cup (120 ml) thin coconut milk, scraping the bottom of the pot to remove any cooked-on bits and avoid the BURN warning.

4 Add the crushed lime leaves, fish sauce, sugar, cabbage and mushrooms and mix everything together. Nestle the tofu pieces in the sauce, taking care not to break them apart. Bathe with the sauce.

5 Lock the lid. Select PRESSURE COOK/MANUAL and set to LOW for 2 minutes. Make sure the steam release valve is sealed. Once pressurized (10 to 15 minutes), the cook cycle will start. When the timer beeps, manually release the pressure. When the float valve drops, press CANCEL and open the lid.

6 Select SAUTÉ and set to MEDIUM/NORMAL. Add the remaining coconut cream and coconut milk, green beans and bell pepper. Stir gently to mix, and cook until crisp-tender, 3 to 5 minutes. Taste and adjust the seasonings. Press CANCEL.

7 Garnish with the shredded lime leaves and serve with steamed rice.

NOTES: If you can't find extra-firm tofu, use baked tofu or tofu puffs. Anything less dense will fall apart in this dish. If you can only find firm tofu, bake it first, or try tempeh or seitan. For a more robust flavor, I prefer to toast whole spices and grind them instead of buying powdered. For this recipe, I used 1½ teaspoons toasted coriander seeds for 1 teaspoon coriander powder and ¾ teaspoon toasted cumin seeds for ½ teaspoon cumin powder.

Lohan Mixed Vegetables

Commonly known as Buddha's Delight or *lo han jai*, this vegetarian dish is eaten on the first day of the Chinese New Year. I've turned it into an everyday dish using some of my favorite vegetables with miso paste added for a truly delicious sauce!

PREP TIME: 15 minutes **TOTAL TIME:** 30 minutes
MAKES: 4 to 6 servings

1 tablespoon vegetable oil

3 tablespoons minced garlic (3 medium cloves)

3 green onions, white parts finely chopped, green parts cut into 2-inch (5-cm) pieces

2 tablespoons white miso

1 large carrot, peeled and cut into 1-inch-thick (2.5-cm) pieces

4 ounces (120 g) fresh or rehydrated (page 37) black mushrooms, halved (save the mushroom soaking water if using dried)

8 ounces (225 g) Chinese cabbage, cored and cut into 2-inch (5-cm) squares

8 ounces (225 g) firm tofu, cut into 1-inch (2.5-cm) squares or triangles

2 dried tofu sheets, broken into 2-inch pieces, soaked for 15 minutes in warm water and drained (2 ounces/60 g)

2 tablespoons soy sauce

1 teaspoon sugar

½ teaspoon fine sea salt

1 small bundle (1 ounce/30 g) mung bean noodles cut into shorter pieces

1 cup mushroom soaking water or water

1 teaspoon sesame oil

NOTES: White miso or *shiro miso* is made from soybeans that have been fermented with a large percentage of rice. The actual resulting color can range from white to light beige, and the miso has a definite sweet taste. Use more soy sauce or salt if you prefer not to use it.

Other than Chinese cabbage, bok choy, chrysanthemum greens or other leafy Chinese greens would be great in this dish. Snow peas too!

If you can't find dried tofu sheets, use more firm tofu or tofu puffs.

1 Select SAUTÉ and set to MEDIUM/NORMAL. Add the vegetable oil. When the pot is hot, add the garlic and the white portions of the green onions. Stir and cook until fragrant, 30 seconds. Add the miso paste and stir and cook for 30 seconds. Add the carrot, cabbage and mushrooms, stirring between each addition. Stir and cook for 1 minute. Press CANCEL.

2 Add the soy sauce, sugar and mushroom water. Stir to mix, scraping the bottom of the pot to remove any cooked-on bits and avoid the BURN warning.

3 Add the tofu skin and mung bean noodles and mix everything together. Make sure the noodles are covered. Lock the lid. Select PRESSURE COOK/MANUAL and set the pressure to HIGH for 2 minutes. Make sure the steam release valve is sealed. Once pressurized (8 to 10 minutes), the cook cycle will start. When the timer beeps, manually release the pressure. When the float valve drops, press CANCEL and open the lid.

4 Add the sesame oil and remaining green onions. Stir for 1 to 2 minutes until the sauce reduces a little. There should be some sauce left, and it will thicken on standing. Serve immediately with steamed rice.

Spiced Cauliflower and Potatoes Aloo Gobi

Quick and easy, this dish takes just 30 minutes from start to finish. Plus, it's vegan and gluten-free! The key is to cook the potatoes first and cut the cauliflower into large florets (larger than the potatoes) so they cook at the same rate.

PREP TIME: 15 minutes TOTAL TIME: 30 minutes
MAKES: 4 to 6 servings as part of a multicourse meal

BRINE
2 tablespoons ghee or vegetable oil
1 teaspoon whole cumin seeds
1 jalapeno, slit open (optional)
½ cup (120 g) finely chopped onion
1 tablespoon minced garlic (3 medium cloves)
1 tablespoon minced fresh ginger
8 ounces (225 g) new potatoes (or other waxy potatoes), peeled and cut into 1-inch (2.5-cm) cubes (about 1 cup)
1 cup (120 g) chopped Roma tomatoes
1 teaspoon ground coriander
½ teaspoon ground turmeric
½ teaspoon red chili powder or cayenne
4 cups cauliflower, cut into large florets (about 1¼ pounds/600 g)
1 teaspoon fine sea salt
1 teaspoon granulated sugar

TO FINISH
¾ teaspoon store-bought garam masala (or make your own: ¼ teaspoon ground cloves, ¼ teaspoon ground cinnamon, ½ teaspoon ground cardamom)
1 tablespoon fresh lemon or lime juice
Handful of cilantro/coriander sprigs, to garnish

> **NOTES:** If the curry sauce looks too watery, remove the cauliflower and potatoes and reduce the sauce on SAUTÉ mode as desired.
>
> If you can't find whole cumin seeds, use 1¼ teaspoons ground cumin, and stir and cook until fragrant.
>
> If you want a little more heat, add more chili powder.
>
> If you prefer your cauliflower firmer, cook on LOW PRESSURE for 1 minute.

1 Select SAUTÉ and set to MEDIUM/NORMAL. Add the ghee. When the pot is hot, add the cumin seeds and jalapeno, if using, and stir and cook until the seeds pop, about 30 seconds to 1 minute.

2 Add the onion, and stir and cook until soft, 2 to 3 minutes. Stir in the garlic and ginger and cook until fragrant, about 30 seconds. Add the potatoes, and stir and cook until golden, 2 to 3 minutes. Tip in the tomatoes. Stir the coriander, turmeric and chili powder. Stir until the tomatoes release their juices. Press CANCEL.

3 Add the cauliflower, salt and sugar. Stir and cook, scraping the bottom of the pot to remove any cooked-on bits and avoid the BURN warning. Add a tablespoon or two of water to loosen if the pot looks too dry.

4 Lock the lid. Select PRESSURE COOK/MANUAL and set the pressure to LOW for 2 minutes. Make sure the steam release valve is sealed. Once pressurized (8 to 10 minutes), the cook cycle will start. When the timer beeps, manually release the pressure. When the float valve drops, press CANCEL and open the lid.

5 Stir in the garam masala. Taste and add more seasonings if desired.

6 Squeeze in the lemon juice and sprinkle with cilantro/coriander leaves just before serving. Serve with naan or basmati rice.

Curried Lentils with Dates & Caramelized Onions

This dish is my riff on *masoor dal* made with split red lentils, a favorite of mine. But you can use other types of lentils or split peas. Dals are often topped with a *tadka* (or *tarka*), a finishing flourish of ghee and spices. It's not authentic, but I've chosen to use spiced caramelized onions as a topping instead.

PREP TIME: 5 minutes (not including caramelizing onions) **TOTAL TIME:** 41 minutes
MAKES: 4 to 6 servings

1 cup (200 g) red lentils, rinsed and picked over
¼ cup pitted dates, chopped (50 g)
3 medium cloves garlic, smashed and peeled
1-inch (2.5-cm) knob ginger, sliced
4½ cups (1.2 l) water
½ teaspoon ground turmeric powder
½ teaspoon ground cumin
1½ teaspoons fine sea salt
Spiced Caramelized Onions (recipe below)
Chopped cilantro/coriander leaves, to garnish

1   Combine the lentils, dates, garlic, ginger and water in the Instant Pot®. Stir in the turmeric, cumin and salt.

2   Lock the lid. Select PRESSURE COOK/ MANUAL and set to HIGH for 6 minutes. Make sure the steam release valve is sealed. Once pressurized (10 to 12 minutes), the cook cycle will start. When the timer beeps, let the pressure release naturally (20 minutes). When the float valve drops, press CANCEL and open the lid. If you'd like your dal soupier, add more water.

3   Stir in the **Spiced Caramelized Onions**. Shower with chopped cilantro/coriander leaves and serve with basmati rice.

> **NOTES:** It's fine to keep the dal on the "Keep Warm" function while the onions finish cooking.

Spiced Caramelized Onions

Start caramelizing the onions before you begin cooking the lentils.

PREP TIME: 5 minutes **COOK TIME:** 35 minutes

¼ cup (60 g) ghee or butter
1 large onion, sliced (1½ cups/150 g)
Fine sea salt
½ teaspoon ground cumin
½ teaspoon ground coriander
¼ teaspoon cayenne or other red chili powder
¼ teaspoon garam masala

1   Heat the ghee in a wide, medium saucepan over medium heat. When melted, add the onion and cook until soft. Sprinkle a pinch of salt and continue cooking until onions are a rich, dark brown, 35 to 45 minutes. Stir and scrape the bottom of the pan occasionally to prevent sticking, and/or add water to prevent from burning.

2   When the onion looks just about ready, add the cumin, coriander and cayenne and stir and cook until aromatic, 1 to 2 minutes. Turn off the heat and stir in the garam masala. Stir the caramelized onions into the cooked pot of lentils.

Spicy Chickpeas in Tomato Sauce — Chana Masala

Dried chickpeas usually need to be soaked for at least 4 hours or overnight before cooking them. But with the Instant Pot®, that isn't necessary. So even if you haven't planned ahead, you can still have this dish on the table within an hour and a half. Or just used canned chickpeas—for an even shorter cooking time.

PREP TIME: 5 minutes   TOTAL TIME: 130 minutes
MAKES: 4 to 6 servings

1 cup (200 g) dried chickpeas, rinsed, sorted and picked over
1 tablespoon vegetable oil
1 cup (225 g) finely chopped onion
1 green chili or jalapeno, slit open
2 teaspoons minced garlic
2 teaspoons grated fresh ginger
¾ teaspoon ground coriander
¾ teaspoon ground cumin
¼ teaspoon ground turmeric
1 can (14½ oz/411 g) diced tomatoes, or 2 cups (450 g) chopped fresh tomatoes
2 cups (500 ml) water
1 teaspoon fine sea salt
1 teaspoon garam masala
¼ teaspoon red chili powder

TO FINISH
½ teaspoon dried mango powder (*amchur*) or lemon juice
Chopped cilantro/coriander leaves, to garnish

> **NOTES:** When using canned chickpeas, use two 15.5-ounce (450-g) cans, drain and rinse before using. Reduce cooking time to 10 minutes and use 1 cup water. When using soaked chickpeas (soak for at least 4 hours), reduce cooking time to 35 minutes.
>
> When cooking with soaked chickpeas, you can cook brown rice using the pot-in-pot method (page 12). Brown rice takes about 25 to 35 minutes to cook PIP, so the two would cook well together.

1 Select SAUTÉ and set to HIGH/MORE. Add the vegetable oil. When the pot is hot, add the onion and green chili and stir and cook until the onion has softened, 2 to 3 minutes.

2 Add the garlic and ginger and stir and cook until fragrant, about 30 seconds. Add the coriander, cumin and turmeric and stir and cook for 30 seconds. Add the tomatoes and water, and scrape the bottom of the pot to remove any cooked-on bits and avoid the BURN warning.

3 Add the chickpeas followed by the salt, garam masala and red chili powder. Stir to mix. Press CANCEL.

4 Lock the lid. Select PRESSURE COOK/ MANUAL and set to HIGH for 55 minutes.

(See notes for more options). Make sure the steam release valve is sealed. Once pressurized (10 to 12 minutes), the cook cycle will start. When the timer beeps, let the pressure release naturally (30 to 40 minutes). If you're in a hurry, quick release after 20 minutes. When the float valve drops, press CANCEL and open the lid.

5 Test a chickpea for doneness. If it's not done to your liking, cook on HIGH PRESSURE for another 5 minutes. Then quick release the pressure.

6 Mix in the mango powder or lemon juice and adjust seasonings as desired. Garnish with cilantro/coriander leaves and serve with basmati rice or naan.

Kimchi Tofu Stew Soondubu Jjigae

This stew is often made with pork or beef, but I enjoy it vegan—its spicy profile has all
the flavor I need. If you can't find all of the ingredients and/or want to scale down for
less heat, instead of 2 tablespoons gochujang, use 1 tablespoon miso.

PREP TIME: 10 minutes **TOTAL TIME:** 30 minutes
MAKES: 4 to 6 servings

1 tablespoon vegetable oil
1 cup (120 g) sliced onion
1 tablespoon minced garlic (3 medium
   cloves)
2 cups (300 g) kimchi, drained, juice
   reserved
1 small zucchini, sliced into ½-inch-
   thick (1.25-cm) moons (1 cup)
4 ounces (120 g) daikon radish sliced
   into ½-inch-thick (1.25-cm) half-
   moons or triangles (¾ cup)
2 ounces (60 g) beech, enoki or other
   small mushrooms
2 tablespoons gochujang
1 tablespoon gochugaru
¼ cup (60 ml) soy sauce
2 teaspoons sesame oil
3 cups (720 ml) low-sodium chicken or
   vegetable stock
1 teaspoon fine sea salt
1 teaspoon granulated sugar
1 (12-ounce/360-g) silken or soft tofu
2 large eggs (optional)
2 green onions, finely chopped

> **NOTES:** While this dish is named for the
> tofu used, if you can't find silken or soft
> tofu, use whatever tofu you can find.

1 Select SAUTÉ and set to MEDIUM/NOR-MAL. Add the vegetable oil. When the pot is hot, add the onion and garlic and stir and cook until aromatic, about 30 seconds. Add the kimchi and cook and stir until the onion softens and turns translucent. Add the zucchini, daikon and the mushrooms and stir and cook for 1 minute. Press CANCEL.

2 Mix together the gochujang and ½ cup (120 ml) stock to form a smooth paste. Add the gochujang paste, gochugaru, soy sauce, sesame oil, kimchi juice, salt and sugar to the pot. Pour in the remaining 2½ cups stock (600 ml). Slide the tofu into the soup and gently break it apart into large pieces.

3 Lock the lid. Select PRESSURE COOK/MANUAL and set to HIGH for 0 minutes. Make sure the steam release valve is sealed. Once pressurized (12 to 15 minutes), the cook cycle will start. When the timer beeps, let the pressure release naturally for 5 minutes. Then quick release any remaining pressure. When the float valve drops, press CANCEL and open the lid.

4 Crack the eggs into the stew, if using, and cook for 1 minute. If your stew is no longer bubbling hot, select SAUTÉ and finish cooking the eggs. Stir and garnish with green onions. Serve immediately with steamed rice.

Baby Eggplant Curry
Bhaingan Bharta

Baby eggplants have thinner skins, making them ideal for stews and curries. They can be short and stout or elongated and narrow, averaging only 1 to 1½ inch (2.5 to 3.75 cm) in length. If you can't find baby eggplant, use the smallest-sized eggplants available and use your judgment to halve or cut them into quarters as needed.

PREP TIME: 5 minutes **TOTAL TIME:** 20 minutes
MAKES: 4 to 6 servings as part of a multicourse meal

1 pound (450 g) baby eggplant (4 to 5)
1 teaspoon ground turmeric
2 teaspoons fine sea salt, divided

SPICE PASTE
2 tablespoons toasted sesame seeds
¼ cup (25 g) unsweetened finely
    shredded coconut
2 medium garlic cloves, peeled
2-inch (5-cm) knob fresh ginger, peeled
2 tablespoons light brown sugar
1 tablespoon tamarind extract (page 18)
2 tablespoons vegetable oil
1 cup (225 g) chopped onion
2 teaspoons ground cumin
2 teaspoons ground coriander
1 teaspoon red chili powder, or to taste
½ cup (120 ml) water, divided

TO FINISH
1 teaspoon sesame oil
Toasted sesame seeds, to garnish
Chopped cilantro/coriander leaves,
    to garnish

NOTES: If you can, let the eggplant curry sit for at least a few hours to allow the flavors to meld.

1 Trim each baby eggplant and cut into quarters. Toss the eggplant with the turmeric and 1 teaspoon salt in a colander over the sink. Leave to sit until needed.

2 Make the spice paste. Blitz the sesame seeds, shredded coconut, garlic, ginger, brown sugar and tamarind extract in a small food processor until a coarse paste forms, 1 to 2 minutes. Add water to loosen the paste if necessary.

3 Select SAUTÉ and set to MEDIUM/NORMAL. Add the vegetable oil. When the pot is hot, add the onion and stir and cook until it softens and turns translucent, 3 to 4 minutes.

4 Add the cumin, coriander, red chili powder and 1 teaspoon salt and stir for 30 seconds until fragrant. Add the spice paste and stir and cook until the onion starts to brown. Press CANCEL. Pour in ½ cup water (or what's left), scraping the bottom of the

pot to remove any stuck-on bits and prevent the BURN warning.

5 Tip the eggplant into the pot. Mix well to coat. Lock the lid. Select PRESSURE COOK/MANUAL and set to HIGH for 2 minutes. Make sure the steam release valve is sealed. Once pressurized (7 to 9 minutes), the cook cycle will start. When the timer beeps, manually release the pressure. When the float valve drops, press CANCEL and open the lid.

6 If you'd like to reduce the sauce, select SAUTÉ and set to MEDIUM/NORMAL. Stir for 2 to 3 minutes until the sauce is reduced to your liking.

7 Drizzle with sesame oil and sprinkle with sesame seeds and cilantro/coriander leaves. Serve at room temperature with basmati rice, store-bought naan or Indian Chicken Biryani Rice (page 48).

One-Dish Meals for a Crowd

One-dish meals are fabulous when you're expecting company. These recipes easily feed a crowd and are a little fancier than your everyday fried rice. Many of the recipes traditionally require hours of prep but thanks to the Instant Pot®, you'll have the meal ready in half the time.

Indian Chicken Biryani Rice

I highly recommend using whole spices in this dish for a more robust flavor. But if you don't fancy biting into a peppercorn or clove, you can always grind the spices first.

PREP TIME: 15 minutes TOTAL TIME: 50 minutes
MAKES: 4 to 6 servings

1 pound (450 g) boneless, skinless chicken breasts or thighs, cut into 1-inch (2.5-cm) pieces
1½ cups (600 g) basmati rice
Large pinch saffron threads
¼ cup (60 ml) just-boiled water
2 to 3 tablespoons ghee or butter
1 large onion, sliced (1½ cups/150 g)
1½ teaspoons fine sea salt
1½ cups (360 ml) low sodium chicken stock
2 cups (240 g) frozen veggies (I use 1 cup corn and 1 cup peas)

MARINADE
1 teaspoon ground cumin
½ teaspoon ground coriander
½ teaspoon red chili powder (optional)
½ teaspoon garam masala
2 tablespoons grated fresh ginger,
2 tablespoons minced garlic, divided (6 medium cloves)
1 teaspoon fine sea salt
2 tablespoons chopped cilantro/coriander leaves, stems and leaves
¼ cup (60 g) plain, full-fat yogurt

WHOLE SPICES
5 black peppercorns
4 whole cloves
5 green cardamom pods
3-inch (7.5-cm) cinnamon stick

TO FINISH
½ cup (75 g) raisins, soaked in water for 10 minutes and dried with a paper towel
Raita (see inset at right)

1 Make the marinade. Mix together the cumin, coriander, chili powder (if using), garam masala, salt, 1 tablespoon ginger, 1 tablespoon garlic, cilantro/coriander leaves and yogurt in a large bowl. Add the chicken and coat evenly with the marinade. Refrigerate for at least 30 minutes.

2 Rinse the rice several times until the water runs clear. Soak until required.

3 Soak the saffron threads in just-boiled water until required.

4 Select SAUTÉ and set to HIGH/MORE. Add 2 tablespoons ghee. When the pot is hot, add the onions and stir and cook until lightly caramelized, 8 to 10 minutes. Scoop out about half the caramelized onions for garnish.

5 Add 1 more tablespoon of ghee. When the ghee has melted, add the remaining 1 tablespoon of ginger and 1 tablespoon of garlic, and cook for 30 seconds. Stir in the whole spices. Add 1½ teaspoons salt and stir for 30 to 45 seconds.

6 Pour in ¼ cup (60 ml) stock and scrape the bottom of the pot to remove any cooked-on bits and avoid the BURN warning.

7 Tip in the chicken plus any juices and leftover marinade. Stir and cook until the chicken sears a little on all sides, 3 to 4 minutes. Don't worry if the chicken is still a little pink. But do scrape the bottom of the pot! Press CANCEL.

8 Drain the rice and tip into the pot over the chicken. Don't mix! Add the remaining 1¼ cups (300 ml) stock, and submerge the rice as much as possible.

9 Lock the lid. Select PRESSURE COOK/ MANUAL and set to HIGH for 5 minutes. Make sure the steam release valve is sealed. Once pressurized (9 to 12 minutes), the cook cycle will start. When the timer beeps, let the pressure release naturally for 10 minutes. Then quick release any remaining pressure. When the float valve drops, press CANCEL and open the lid.

10 Add the vegetables and gently mix everything together gently with a wooden or silicon spatula to prevent the rice grains from breaking. Let the vegetables cook in the residual heat for 2 to 3 minutes.

11 Spoon the chicken, vegetables and rice into a large, shallow serving bowl. Pick out the whole spices. Drizzle the saffron liquid, including threads, over the rice. Garnish with the remaining caramelized onions and raisins. Serve with Raita and store-bought chutney.

> **RAITA:** Mix together 2 cups (450 g) yogurt, ½ teaspoon cumin powder and a pinch of sea salt in a small bowl with a fork until the yogurt is smooth and there are no lumps.

NOTES: You can mince the garlic and ginger at the same time in a food processor.

My friend Samia who shared this recipe with me, recommends buying free-range, organic chicken breasts because they have not been injected with saline. You don't want a watery biryani.

It's normal for the top layer of the rice to look a bit undercooked. Simply fluff the top layer and then gently mix the biryani.

This recipe makes a medium-spicy biryani. For extra-spicy biryani, toss in one to two sliced jalapenos when you add the whole spices.

To speed up the cooking process, you can also caramelize the onions in a nonstick pan on the stovetop. This will also lower your chances of getting a BURN notice.

My recipe tester Debra suggests using a spice sachet to hold the whole spices to make it easier to remove them.

Vietnamese Chicken Noodle Soup Pho Ga

Ever-thrifty, I always have chicken bones in the freezer and I put them to good use in this pho recipe. You can also use all bone-in chicken thighs and drumsticks, or a whole chicken (say 3 to 4 pounds/1.5 to 2 kg), and set aside half the chicken meat for another use.

PREP TIME: 15 minutes **TOTAL TIME:** 1 hour, 35 minutes **MAKES:** 4 to 6 servings

SOUP INGREDIENTS
2 tablespoons vegetable oil
2 medium onions, peeled and quartered
3-inch (7.5-cm) knob ginger, peeled and roughly sliced
3 medium garlic cloves, peeled and smashed
1 tablespoon coriander seeds
1 teaspoon black peppercorns
1 teaspoon fennel seeds
1 teaspoon 5-spice powder (optional, or use whole spices, see note below)
1 heaped tablespoon goji berries or 5 small dates, pitted (optional)
1 small bunch cilantro/coriander leaves and stems, tied with kitchen twine
1½ pounds (720 g) bone-in chicken thighs
1½ pounds (720 g) chicken bones (backs, necks and wings are great)
8 cups (2 l) water
¼ cup (60 ml) fish sauce
1 to 2 tablespoons granulated sugar
1½ teaspoons fine sea salt

TO SERVE
8 ounces (240 g) dried rice noodles (size: S [1mm]), prepared according to the package directions
1 cup (120 g) thinly sliced onion, soaked in water to remove their bite
¼ cup (60 g) chopped green onions, green and white parts
2 cups (50 g) mixed herbs (cilantro/coriander leaves, Thai basil and mint)
2 cups (200 g) trimmed mung bean sprouts
2 jalapenos, thinly sliced
2 limes, each cut into 4 wedges
Hoisin sauce
Sriracha or other chili sauce

1 Select SAUTÉ and set to HIGH/MORE. Add the vegetable oil. When the pot is hot, add the onions and ginger. Cook, stirring occasionally until they are nicely charred, about 10 minutes. Adjust to MEDIUM/NORMAL if it starts smoking excessively. If you're in a hurry, you can cut this part short.

2 Add the garlic, coriander, black peppercorns fennel seeds, and 5-spice powder, if using. Stir and cook until fragrant, 1 to 2 minutes. Add the goji berries, cilantro, bone-in chicken and bones to the pot. Add 8 cups (2 l) water. Stir in the fish sauce, sugar and salt. Press CANCEL.

3 Lock the lid. Select PRESSURE COOK/MANUAL and set to HIGH for 15 minutes. Make sure the steam release valve is sealed. Once pressurized (25 to 30 minutes), the cook cycle will start. When the timer beeps, let the pressure release naturally for 20 minutes. If the float valve hasn't dropped by this time, quick release any remaining pressure. When the float valve drops, press CANCEL and open the lid.

4 Transfer the chicken thighs to a plate with tongs. Pour the soup through a fine mesh strainer into a clean pot and discard the solids. Or scoop up the solids with a slotted spoon or spider from the soup. (You can make the broth up to 2 days ahead and refrigerate until ready to eat.)

5 Skim off any residue and some (not all!) fat from the surface of the broth using a ladle. Taste and adjust seasonings with more fish sauce and sugar if desired. You should end up with 7 to 8 cups of soup.

6 Cut or shred the chicken meat into bite-sized pieces. Discard the skin. (The chicken can be refrigerated for up to 3 days or frozen for up to 3 months.)

7 Simmer the soup over medium heat as you assemble the bowls.

8 To serve, place the noodles in individual noodle bowls. Top with chicken, sliced onions and green onions. Pour about 1½ to 2 cups (480 ml) hot soup over the noodles. Serve immediately, passing herbs, bean sprouts, jalapenos, limes and sauces at the table.

> **NOTES:** Feel free to add star anise (2 pods), cloves (4), cinnamon (2-inch/5-cm stick) and/or cardamom (3 pods) to the spice mixture, if you'd like.
>
> My recipe tester Elizabeth suggests buying spices (and other dried goods like goji berries and dates) in the bulk section whenever possible. You'll save money and you won't end up with too much of a spice you might not use before it loses its potency.
>
> Elizabeth also likes the idea of making this dish for a small dinner party. "I always like to serve things that have options for customizing your plate to suit your needs."

Hainanese Chicken Rice

Hainanese chicken rice is a very popular dish in Singapore and Malaysia. In Thailand, a similar dish is called *khao man gai*. It is deceptively simple and relies heavily on the main ingredient—chicken. The key is to purchase good quality chicken. Organic is good, as is air-chilled chicken. Air-chilled chicken has drier skin and it's not injected with saline.

PREP TIME: 30 minutes **TOTAL TIME:** 1 hour, 20 minutes **MAKES:** 4 to 6 servings

THE CHICKEN
1 (3½ pounds/1.8 kg) whole chicken, trimmed of fat (reserve the fat)
1 tablespoon fine sea salt
4-inch (10-cm) knob fresh ginger, peeled and sliced into coins
3 green onions, trimmed
8 cups (2 l) water
2 teaspoons sesame oil

THE RICE
2 tablespoons vegetable oil
1½ tablespoons minced garlic (4 medium cloves)
1 tablespoon minced fresh ginger
1 tablespoon finely chopped shallot
2 cups (400 g) jasmine or other long-grain rice, rinsed in several changes of water until the water runs clear
2 cups (480 ml) reserved chicken stock
1 teaspoon fine sea salt
2 pandan leaves tied together into a knot

THE SOUP
3 cups (720 ml) chicken stock
1 cup (240 ml) water
½ cup shredded lettuce or cabbage
½ teaspoon fine sea salt or soy sauce, or to taste
Chopped green onions, to garnish

TO SERVE
Chili sauce (page 53)
Ginger sauce (page 53)
Sweet soy sauce (page 53)

TO FINISH
2 teaspoons sesame oil
2 teaspoons soy sauce
1 bunch fresh cilantro/coriander leaves, leaves
2 large cucumbers, peeled and sliced

SPECIAL EQUIPMENT
Mixing bowl large enough to fit the whole chicken
Strainer

POACH THE CHICKEN

1 Pat the chicken dry with paper towels. Massage the sea salt all over the chicken, and inside the cavity. Stuff the ginger and green onions into the cavity.

2 Place the chicken in the pot breast-side down, and pour in enough water to cover the chicken by ½ inch (1.25 cm) or to reach maximum level, 8 to 10 cups.

3 Lock the lid. Select PRESSURE COOK/ MANUAL and set to HIGH for 0 minutes. Make sure the steam release valve is sealed. Once pressurized (25 to 35 minutes), the cook cycle will start.

4 When the chicken is almost done poaching, fill a large bowl with ice water.

5 When the timer beeps, let the pressure release naturally for 20 minutes. Then quick release any remaining pressure. When the float valve drops, press CANCEL and open the lid.

6 Insert a meat thermometer into the thigh. The temperature should read at least 165°F (74°C). If the temperature reads below 165°F, close the lid for a few more minutes and let the chicken cook in the residual heat. Check the temperature again.

7 When the chicken is cooked, lift it from the pot with tongs and let the liquid drain out from its cavity. Dunk the chicken in the ice water for 10 to 15 minutes. This will stop the cooking process and produce tender meat and firm skin.

8 Place the chicken on a cutting board and pat dry with paper towels. Rub sesame oil into the skin to prevent it from drying out.

9 Pour the poaching liquid through a fine mesh strainer into a large bowl and discard the solids. Reserve the chicken stock for later use.

COOK THE RICE

1 Once the chicken is done, rinse and dry the Instant Pot to cook the rice.

2 Select SAUTÉ and set to HIGH/MORE. Add the reserved chicken fat. When the pot is hot and the fat has rendered, add the garlic, ginger and shallot and stir and cook until fragrant, about 30 seconds. (If you get less than 1 tablespoon of rendered fat, add vegetable oil). Remove the solid fat. Add the rice, and stir to coat.

3 Add about ¼ cup (60 ml) stock and scrape the bottom of the pot to remove any cooked-on bits and avoid the BURN warning. Pour in the remaining 1¾ cups (420 ml) stock, and add 1 teaspoon salt and the pandan leaves.

4 Lock the lid. Select PRESSURE COOK/ MANUAL and set to HIGH for 3 minutes. Make sure the steam release valve is sealed. Once pressurized (10 to 15 minutes), the cook cycle will start. When the timer beeps, manually release the pressure. When the float valve drops, press CANCEL and open the lid. Fluff the rice with a fork.

MAKE THE SOUP

Heat the chicken stock and water in a medium saucepan. Bring to a gentle boil and blanch the lettuce for about 1 minute. Season with salt or soy sauce to taste.

TO SERVE

1 Cut the chicken into bite-sized pieces, either Asian-Style with the bones, or Western-Style without. Arrange the pieces on a large serving platter just like a roast turkey. Drizzle the sesame oil and soy sauce over the chicken.

2 Garnish with cilantro/coriander leaves and cucumbers on the side.

3 Scoop rice onto 4 to 6 plates.

4 Ladle soup into small soup bowls and sprinkle with green onions.

5 Serve the chicken with plates of rice, soup and Sauces to pass at the table (see below). To eat, drizzle one or all of the sauces over the rice. Dip a piece of chicken into one or all the sauces and eat together with a spoonful of rice.

MAKE THE SAUCES

After the rice is prepped, start making all the sauces and stop at the point where you add the stock. The sauces can also be made ahead and refrigerated for 3 days.

CHILI

5 medium garlic cloves, smashed and peeled
1-inch (2.5-cm) knob fresh ginger, peeled and roughly chopped
6 tablespoons reserved chicken stock
¼ cup (60 ml) chili paste like *sambal oelek*
2 tablespoons lime juice (preferably key limes or *calamansi*)
2 teaspoons sugar

Blitz the garlic, ginger, stock, chili paste, lime juice and sugar in a food processor until smooth. Taste and adjust seasonings if desired.

GINGER

2 ounces (60 g) fresh ginger, peeled and roughly chopped
3 tablespoons chicken stock
1 tablespoon vegetable oil
¼ teaspoon sesame oil
½ teaspoon granulated sugar
¼ teaspoon fine sea salt

Blitz the ginger in a food processor. Whisk together with the stock, vegetable oil, sesame oil, sugar and salt. Taste and adjust seasonings if desired.

SWEET SOY

¼ cup (60 ml) hot reserved chicken stock
2 tablespoons granulated sugar
3 tablespoons dark soy sauce

Whisk together the stock and sugar until the sugar has dissolved completely. Microwave on low if necessary to dissolve the sugar completely. Mix in the dark soy sauce.

Vietnamese Meatballs with Rice Noodles   Bun Cha

There are several ways to serve this dish, either everything in one bowl or as separate components—the choice is yours. Ground chicken, turkey or beef are acceptable substitutes for the meatballs, but always release the pressure naturally for at least 10 minutes to ensure soft, tender meatballs.

PREP TIME: 20 minutes TOTAL TIME: 45 minutes
MAKES: 4 servings

MEATBALLS
1 pound (450 g) ground pork
1 tablespoon minced lemongrass (from 1 plump stalk, prepped, page 58)
1 tablespoon minced garlic (3 medium cloves)
¼ cup finely chopped shallots
1 tablespoon chopped cilantro/coriander leaves
1 tablespoon cornstarch
1 teaspoon salt
¾ teaspoon granulated sugar
⅛ teaspoon freshly ground black pepper
2 tablespoons vegetable oil

SAUCE
¼ cup (60 ml) lime juice (from 2 large limes)
3 tablespoons fish sauce
½ cup (120 ml) water
¼ cup (50 g) granulated sugar
2 teaspoons chili paste like *sambal oelek*, or to taste

TO SERVE
2 cups (110 g) shredded iceberg, romaine or butter lettuce
8 ounces (240 g) dried rice vermicelli noodles, cooked according to package directions, drained and rinsed under cold water
½ cup carrot cut into matchsticks (2 ounces/60 g)
½ cup (120 g) sliced onion (optional)
2 cups (50 g) loosely packed herbs like mint, Thai basil and cilantro/coriander leaves
Crushed roasted peanuts (optional)
Crushed dried chilies (optional)
2 limes cut into wedges

SPECIAL EQUIPMENT
Parchment paper
Large rimmed baking tray

1   Make the meatballs. Mix together the pork, lemongrass, garlic, shallots, cilantro, cornstarch, salt, sugar and pepper in a large bowl. Roll into 16 (1-inch/2.5-cm) meatballs and place on a parchment-lined baking tray.

2   Select SAUTÉ and set to HIGH/MORE. Add the oil. When the pot is hot, arrange the meatballs in one layer in the pressure cooker. Sear for 4 to 5 minutes before flipping over carefully and scraping up any browned bits. Flatten the meatballs a little. Sear for 2 to 3 minutes on this side. Press CANCEL.

3   Make the sauce. Mix together the lime juice, fish sauce, water, sugar and chili paste. You'll have about 1 cup (240 ml). Mix

⅓ cup (80ml) sauce with ⅓ cup (80 ml) water and pour into the pressure cooker (reserve the remaining ⅔ cup/160 ml sauce to pass around the table). Scrape the bottom of the pot to loosen the meatballs and remove any cooked-on bits and avoid the BURN warning. (If you find it hard to scrape the pot with the browned meatballs inside, remove them to a plate. Pour in the sauce, scrape, then return the meatballs to the pot.)

4   Lock the lid. Select PRESSURE COOK/MANUAL and set to HIGH for 5 minutes. Make sure the steam release valve is sealed. Once pressurized (4 to 6 minutes), the cook cycle will start.

5   While the meatballs are cooking, divide the lettuce among 4 bowls. Top with noodles. Arrange the carrot, onion (if using), herbs, crushed peanuts, crushed chilies (if using) and lime wedges on a large platter or in several small serving dishes. Or distribute among the bowls.

6   When the timer beeps, let the pressure release naturally for 10 minutes. Then quick release any remaining pressure. When the float valve drops, press CANCEL and open the lid. Place 4 meatballs on top of each bowl of noodles. Serve with remaining ⅔ cup (160 ml) sauce and vegetables to pass around the table.

7   To eat, pour 2 to 3 tablespoons of sauce over the noodles, or dip the noodles into the sauce served in little bowls. Each bite should have a little meatball, noodles, vegetables and herbs.

HOW TO MAKE THE MEATBALLS

NOTES: In addition to, or instead of, the carrots, you can use daikon radish, cucumbers, kohlrabi, green papaya or bean sprouts. Serve pickled vegetables if you'd like.

NOTES: Traditionally, this dish is served with bone-in thighs and/or drumsticks. If drumsticks are on sale, buy as many as the number of people you want to feed (4 or 6). Increase the cooking time to 20 minutes.

Thai Red Curry Chicken Noodles   Khao Soi

Khao soi is a popular northern Thai noodle dish. Traditionally, this dish is served with egg noodles but feel free to use rice noodles for a gluten-free option.

**PREP TIME: 15 minutes TOTAL TIME: 55 minutes
MAKES: 4 to 6 bowls**

CURRY GRAVY

2 tablespoons vegetable oil
1 tablespoon minced garlic (3 medium cloves)
¼ cup (60 g) chopped shallots
¼ cup (60 ml) red curry paste
1 teaspoon ground turmeric
½ teaspoon yellow curry powder or paste
3 tablespoons fish sauce
2 tablespoons soy sauce
3 tablespoons coconut sugar or 2 tablespoons light brown sugar
1 teaspoon fine sea salt
1½ pounds (720 g) boneless, skinless chicken thighs or breasts, cut into bite-sized pieces
2 cups (480 ml) low-sodium chicken stock
1 (13½-ounce/400-ml) can coconut milk

FOR THE BOWLS

8 ounces (240 g) dried or 1 pound (450 g) fresh Chinese egg or wheat noodles
1 cup (240 ml) unsweetened coconut cream (not milk!), gently warmed
Fried Noodle Topping (see recipe to right)
1 cup (140g) chopped Pickled Chinese Mustard Cabbage (page 30), rinsed and drained
1 cup (25 g) chopped cilantro/coriander leaves
½ cup (120 g) sliced shallots or red onions, soaked in water to tame their bite
Limes, halved or cut into wedges (preferably key limes)
Store-bought roasted chili paste
Fish sauce

1 Make the gravy. Select SAUTÉ and set to MEDIUM/NORMAL. Add 2 tablespoons oil. When the pot is hot, add the garlic and shallot and stir and cook until fragrant, about 30 seconds.

2 Add the red curry paste, turmeric and yellow curry powder. Stir to break up the paste. Some of the paste will likely brown and stick to the pot, so scrape the bottom occasionally to make sure it doesn't burn. Add a little stock to loosen, if necessary, and/or adjust the heat to LOW/LESS.

3 When the curry paste turns a few shades darker and your kitchen fills with a pungent aroma, 3 to 4 minutes, add the fish sauce, soy sauce, coconut sugar and salt. Stir and cook until a smooth paste forms.

4 Tip the chicken into the pot and toss to coat with the paste. Stir and cook for about 1 minute to allow the chicken to absorb the flavors a bit. Press CANCEL. Pour in the stock.

5 Lock the lid. Select PRESSURE COOK/MANUAL and set to HIGH for 15 minutes. Make sure the steam release valve is sealed. Once pressurized (7 to 10 minutes), the cook cycle will start. When the timer beeps, let the pressure release naturally (about 20 minutes). When the float valve

drops, press CANCEL and open the lid.

6 See that layer of red oil on the surface? That's a good sign! Stir in the coconut milk and taste. The curry gravy should taste a bit too salty and a tad sweet, with some heat to it. Keep in mind that the flavors will balance out when you add the coconut cream and eat the noodles with the gravy. Adjust the seasonings if desired. Select the WARM function until ready to serve.

7 You can keep the gravy warm on the stove for up to 3 hours or in the fridge for up to 3 days. (It will taste even better as the flavors meld and the meat soaks up the curry.)

8 Assemble the bowls. While the gravy is cooking, bring a large pot of water to a rolling boil. Cook the noodles according to package directions (aim for just shy of al dente, not mushy), 2 to 3 minutes. Drain well. Save about 3 ounces (90 g) of cooked noodles to make the topping and divide the rest equally among 4 to 6 bowls.

9 Ladle about 1 cup (240 ml) of gravy over each bowl. Spoon on 2 tablespoons of the warm coconut cream, and top with a nest of fried noodles. Pass Pickled Chinese Mustard Cabbage, cilantro, shallots, limes, chili paste and fish sauce at the table.

Fried Noodle Topping

Make the topping ahead of time. Once they're cool, store in an airtight container kept in a dry, cool place for a day or two.

3 ounces (90 g) cooked noodles (enough to top 4 to 6 bowls)
Vegetable oil
Rack or paper towels

1 Pour enough oil into a wide medium pot to reach a depth of 2 inches (5 cm) and set the pot over medium-high heat. Heat the oil to 350°F (or test the temperature by dropping a piece of noodle into the oil; it should turn golden brown in about 20 seconds).

2 Pat the noodles dry if necessary. Toss on a plate to separate them so there are no clumps. Divide into 4 to 6 portions.

3 Fry in batches, turning over the nest of noodles once, just until the noodles are golden brown and crunchy, 20 to 45 seconds per batch. Drain on a rack or paper towels.

Fragrant Oxtail Stew

The connective tissues in the oxtail melt into the stew, giving it a silky texture, and the meat itself is very tender and has a slight chewiness. If you prefer, opt for bone-in short ribs, or 2½ pounds (1 kg) grass-fed beef brisket or chuck roast, trimmed and cut into 1½-inch (3.75-cm) cubes.

PREP TIME: 15 mins TOTAL TIME: 2 hours, 15 mins MAKES: 4 to 6 servings

1 Make the marinade. Whisk together the fish sauce, five-spice powder, black pepper, chili powder and minced lemongrass in a large bowl. Tip the oxtails into the bowl and massage with the marinade until each piece is evenly coated. Let sit for at least 15 minutes, longer if time permits.

2 Turn on the broiler in your oven and set the rack 6 inches (15 cm) from the heating element. Arrange the oxtails in a single layer on a rimmed baking sheet covered in foil. Broil for about 5 minutes on each side or until nicely browned.

3 While the oxtails are broiling, select SAUTÉ on your Instant Pot® and set to HIGH/MORE. Add the vegetable oil. When the pot is hot, add the shallots and stir and cook until softened, 3 to 4 minutes. Add the ginger and garlic and cook until fragrant, another 30 seconds. Stir in the tomato paste and cook until the paste darkens, 1 to 2 minutes. Add the chopped tomatoes and stir and cook until softened, 1 to 2 minutes. Press CANCEL.

4 Pour in the coconut water and stock, scraping the bottom of the pot to remove any stuck-on bits. Add the fish sauce, star anise, cinnamon stick and lemongrass stalks. Stir to mix. Nestle the broiled oxtails in the pot. Pour in any juices from the baking sheet.

5 Lock the lid. Select PRESSURE COOK/MANUAL and set to HIGH for 45 minutes. Make sure the steam release valve is sealed. Once pressurized (20 to 30 minutes), the cook cycle will start. When the timer beeps, manually release the pressure. When the float valve drops, press CANCEL and open the lid.

6 Add the root vegetables. Lock the lid. Select PRESSURE COOK/MANUAL and set to HIGH for 5 minutes.

7 When the timer beeps again, let the pressure release naturally for at least 30 minutes. Then quick release any remaining pressure. When the float valve drops, press CANCEL and open the lid. The meat should be tender and falling off the bone.

8 Taste the stew and add ½ to 1 teaspoon salt and more black pepper to taste. Skim off fat from the surface. If you're not planning to eat right away, refrigerate the stew overnight to allow the flavors to meld. The fat will also solidify on the surface making it easy to remove from the surface.

9 Serve with steamed rice, rice noodles or a freshly baked baguette.

3½ to 4 pounds (1.5 to 2 kg) oxtails cut crosswise into 3-inch (7.5 cm) segments
1 tablespoon vegetable oil
1 cup (160 g) sliced shallots or red onion
2 tablespoons minced fresh ginger
1 tablespoon minced garlic (3 cloves)
¼ cup (60 g) tomato paste
1 large tomato, chopped
2 cups (480 ml) pure coconut water
½ cup (120 ml) low-sodium beef or chicken stock
¼ cup (60 ml) fish sauce
3 star anise pods
2 plump lemongrass stalks, prepped (see below), cut into 3-inch (7.5-cm) lengths, and bruised
2-inch (5-cm) cinnamon stick
3 Thai chilies, slit (optional)
1½ pounds (720 g) root vegetables (carrots, turnips, potatoes) peeled and chopped into 1½-inch (4-cm) pieces
Fine sea salt to taste

MARINADE
2 tablespoons fish sauce
2 teaspoons five-spice powder
1 teaspoon freshly ground pepper
1 teaspoon red chili powder (optional)
2 tablespoons minced lemongrass (from 1 plump stalk, see below)

GARNISHES
Chopped green onions
Cilantro/coriander sprigs

SPECIAL EQUIPMENT
Rimmed baking sheet
Foil

HOW TO CUT A LEMONGRASS STALK

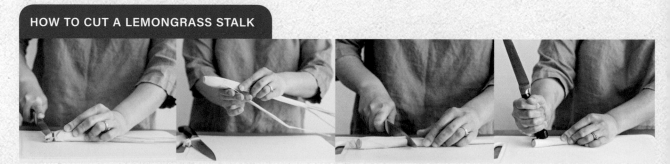

NOTES: You can brown the oxtails in batches in the Instant Pot® on the SAUTÉ function, but I learned a trick from Michelle Tam of Nom Nom Paleo blog fame—broil them! It's not as messy and takes less effort.

If you're not planning to eat right away, refrigerate the stew overnight to allow the flavors to meld. The fat will solidify on the surface, making it easy to remove.

HOW TO MAKE THE STEW

Japanese Shoyu Ramen Noodles

Making ramen the traditional way is a lengthy process. Even the pressure cooker can only streamline the process and shorten cooking time by so much. But your hard work will be rewarded!

PREP TIME: 5 minutes per bowl (not including making toppings) **TOTAL TIME:** 10 minutes per bowl
MAKES: 4 to 6 servings

SOUP

8 ounces (240 g) dried or 1 pound (450 g) fresh ramen noodles
6 to 8 cups (1 to 2 l) pork ramen broth base (page 106), or low-sodium chicken stock
2 to 3 cups (480 to 720 ml) Shoyu Tare Sauce (see below)
Fine sea salt

TO FINISH

Sesame or other flavored oil (like garlic or onion, optional)
Chopped green onions

> **NOTES:** Always add the flavored oil to individual bowls and not directly to the pot of broth. If you boil the broth with the oil in it, it will suspend the fat into the liquid which will make your soup cloudy. You want a nice layer of fat on top of the broth to help insulate it and coat the noodles.

CHOICE OF TOPPINGS PER BOWL

2 slices braised pork belly (page 106)
Half a Japanese-Style Soy Sauce Egg (page 28)
2 to 3 strips seasoned Seasoned Bamboo Shoots (page 29)
2 tablespoons kimchi
1 tablespoon corn kernels (frozen or fresh)
1 sheet toasted *nori* seaweed
Furikake (seaweed and sesame seed mix)
Shichimi togarashi (Japanese seven-spice mix)

SPECIAL EQUIPMENT

Large noodle bowls (I use 3½ cups/840-ml bowls)

1 Before you start, have all your toppings cooked and ready to go.
2 Simmer the ramen broth base in a large pot on the stove over medium heat.
3 Boil your noodles according to package directions, usually 5 to 6 minutes for dried, or 2 to 3 minutes for fresh noodles.
4 Pour 1 cup (240 ml, or more if your bowls are bigger) of broth into each bowl, and whisk in the *tare* by the tablespoon until the flavor of the broth tastes just right for you, ¼ to ⅓ cup (60 to 80 ml). The amount of *tare* you add will depend on your soy sauce and how much your *tare* has reduced. Taste and add salt as desired. The first bowl will help you gauge the amount of *tare* to use. If you are making multiple bowls, remember that it's better to underseason so that individual diners can add more salt as desired.
5 Drain the noodles and divide among the bowls. Drizzle with sesame oil if using, shower with green onions, and tuck your choice of toppings in on the side. Serve immediately and pass *furikake* and *shichimi togarashi*, if using, at the table.

Shoyu Tare Sauce

Tare is a concentrated flavoring sauce that gives ramen its saltiness. But *tare* can do much more than just deliver salt. It can also provide additional umami, sweetness, sourness or spiciness. The basic ingredients are: soy sauce, sake and/or mirin. In addition, anything from tahini (or Chinese sesame paste) to miso, chili flakes or vinegar can be added to perk up the *tare*. There are no hard-and-fast rules, and everything can be adjusted to taste. If you're making Japanese-Style Braised Pork Belly (page 106), you can use the braising liquid as your *tare*. If not, here's a simple recipe.

MAKES: 3½ cups

Place the garlic, ginger, soy sauce, mirin, stock, sake and sugar in a small saucepan and bring to a gentle boil over medium-high heat. Lower the heat and simmer for 5 to 7 minutes.

2 medium cloves garlic, peeled and smashed
2-inch (5-cm) knob fresh ginger, peeled and sliced
1 cup (240 ml) soy sauce
1 cup (240 ml) mirin
1 cup (240 ml) low-sodium chicken stock
½ cup (240 ml) sake or Chinese cooking wine
¼ cup (60 g) granulated sugar

There are several steps to making ramen:
1   Make the ramen broth (page 60)
2   Make the toppings: Braised Pork Belly (page 106),
     Japanese-Style Soy Sauce Eggs (page 28) and
     Seasoned Bamboo Shoots (page 29)
3   Make the *Shoyu Tare Sauce* (page 60)
4   Boil the noodles
5   Assemble the bowls

You can always make the broth and toppings ahead (up to 3 days). When you're ready to eat, all you have to do is assemble the bowls, which takes minutes! However, you can always use shortcuts: store-bought broth and leftovers or easy-to-make toppings save time and effort.

Taiwanese Spicy Beef Noodles

Beef noodles are often considered Taiwan's national dish. This recipe comes courtesy of Linda Shiue, or rather Linda's mother. Linda is a physician who also teaches healthy cooking classes. Even though she's an accomplished cook, she always defers to her mother when it comes to making this dish.

PREP TIME: 15 minutes TOTAL TIME: 1 hour, 20 minutes MAKES: 4 to 6 servings

2 to 2½ pounds (900 g to 1.2 kg) beef chuck roast, cut into 1-inch (2.5-cm) cubes

2 teaspoons fine sea salt

½ teaspoon freshly ground black pepper

2 tablespoons vegetable oil

¾ cup (120 g) chopped onion

3 medium cloves garlic, peeled and smashed

2-inch (5-cm) knob fresh ginger, peeled and cut into ½-inch (1.25-cm) slices

2 medium Roma tomatoes, cut into quarters (4 ounces/120 g)

3 large carrots, peeled and cut into 1½-inch (3.75-cm) pieces (8 ounces/240 g)

½ cup (120 ml) soy sauce

3 tablespoons granulated sugar

WHOLE SPICES
4 black peppercorns
4 Sichuan peppercorns
4 whole cloves
4 star anise pods
1 to 6 dried red chilies, depending on how spicy you like it
Peel of ½ orange or tangerine, or 1 clementine

TO SERVE
8 ounces (240 g) bok choy, Chinese (napa) cabbage or other Chinese greens, chopped
8 ounces (240 g) dried thick Chinese wheat noodles, or 1 pound (450 g) fresh Japanese udon

GARNISHES
Cilantro/coriander leaves
Chopped green onions
Chili sauce
Chopped preserved Chinese vegetables such as Pickled Chinese Mustard Cabbage (page 30) or Sichuan pickles

1 Season the beef with 2 teaspoons salt and ½ teaspoon ground black pepper.

2 Select SAUTÉ and set to HIGH/MORE. Add the oil. When the pot is hot, sear the beef on all sides, 4 to 5 minutes. Don't worry if some pink remains.

3 Add the onion, garlic, and ginger, and stir and cook for another 2 to 3 minutes. Add the tomatoes and carrots and stir and cook. Press CANCEL.

4 Add the soy sauce, scraping the bottom of the pot to remove any cooked-on bits and avoid the BURN warning.

5 Add the sugar and whole spices: black peppercorns, Sichuan peppercorns, cloves, star anise, dried chilies and orange peel. Stir to mix.

6 Lock the lid. Select PRESSURE COOK/MANUAL and set to HIGH for 35 minutes. Make sure the steam release valve is sealed. Once pressurized (8 to 10 minutes), the cook cycle will start.

7 While the beef cooks, bring a large pot of water to a boil. Add the bok choy and blanch for 1 minute. Remove with a spider or slotted spoon and rinse under cold running water.

8 Wait for the water to start boiling again, then cook the noodles according to package directions. Drain and save the noodle cooking liquid.

9 When the timer beeps, let the pressure release naturally for 15 minutes. Then quick release any remaining pressure. When the float valve drops, press CANCEL and open the lid.

10 Fish out the herbs and spices. Skim off fat from the surface. Taste and adjust seasonings as desired. The sauce should taste a little salty.

11 Divide the noodles among 4 to 6 large bowls. Spoon some beef, carrots and sauce over the noodles and top with bok choy. Add some noodle cooking liquid to make it soupier if desired.

12 Garnish with green onions and cilantro sprigs and pass the chili sauce and preserved Chinese vegetables at the table.

> **NOTES:** Udon is a thick wheat noodle that is usually served in soups. Fresh and frozen udon are available at Asian markets.
>
> For a gluten-free option, use gluten-free spaghetti or linguine.
>
> You can also use bone-in beef shanks for this dish. But parboil them first before cooking.
>
> My recipe tester Marcie suggests using a spice sachet to enclose the whole spices and for easy removal, but the flavors may not diffuse as well.

Korean Bibimbap Mixed Rice Bowl

Leftover lovers are presented with a wealth of options when it comes to assembling the contrasting textures and flavors that make up this hodgepodge dish. Here I've suggested you repurpose other Korean dishes in this book. But just about anything goes! The gochujang adds some kick and helps to bring the dish together. If you like your eggs sunny side up, break the yolk and mix it into the rice for a rich and decadent finish.

PREP TIME: 10 minutes TOTAL TIME: 20 minutes (not including toppings) MAKES: 4 servings

1¼ cups carrots, cut in matchsticks
2 cups baby spinach
2 cups bean sprouts
6 cups cooked white rice
4 cups Marinated Pork Bulgogi (page 102), Braised Korean Short Ribs (page 81),
   Korean Glass Noodles (page 68) or a combination
1 cup Quick Cucumber Kimchi (page 31)
1 cup cabbage kimchi (storebought or homemade)
4 large eggs
2 teaspoons sesame oil
Toasted sesame seeds
Gochujang

1 Cook the carrots, spinach and bean sprouts to your liking. Set aside to cool.

2 Assemble the bowls. Scoop 1½ cups cooked rice into each of 4 bowls.

3 Arrange 1 cup pork, short ribs, glass noodles or a combination on top of the rice.

4 Divide the cooked vegetables into 4 portions. Add 1 portion vegetables, ¼ cup Quick Cucumber Kimchi and ¼ cup cabbage kimchi to each bowl.

5 Fry the eggs to taste, either sunny side up or over easy, and place one on top of each bowl.

6 Drizzle with ½ teaspoon sesame oil and sprinkle with toasted sesame seeds.

7 Pass gochujang at the table. Mix in 1 teaspoon to taste, before eating.

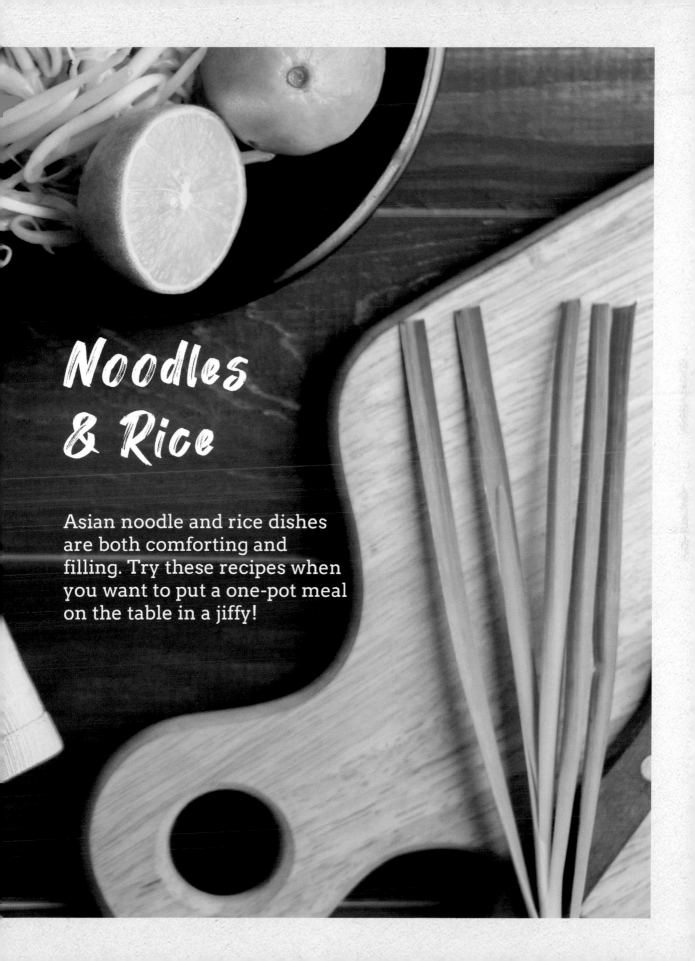

Noodles & Rice

Asian noodle and rice dishes are both comforting and filling. Try these recipes when you want to put a one-pot meal on the table in a jiffy!

Korean Glass Noodles   Japchae

Japchae is perfect for feeding a crowd. It's easy to prepare in bulk and can be served warm or room temperature! Plus, once the ingredients are prepped, this recipe comes together very fast and makes for an easy weeknight dinner.

PREP TIME: 10 minutes **TOTAL TIME:** 25 minutes
MAKES: 4 to 6 servings

1 pound (450 g) dried sweet potato
   noodles
2 tablespoons vegetable oil
1 tablespoon minced garlic (3 medium
   cloves)
1 cup (225 g) sliced onion
3 medium carrots, cut into 2 x ¼ x ¼
   inch (5 cm x 6 mm x 6 mm) batons
   (1½ cups)
4 ounces (120 g) shiitake or other
   meaty mushrooms, sliced
½ cup (120 ml) soy sauce
¼ cup (50 g) light brown sugar
3 tablespoons sesame oil
2 cups (480 ml) low-sodium chicken
   or vegetable stock, plus more as
   needed
1 cup green onions cut into 2-inch
   (5-cm) pieces
4 cups loosely packed baby spinach, or
   chopped spinach (900 g)
Fine sea salt and freshly ground black
   pepper to taste
Toasted sesame seeds, for garnish

> **NOTES:** Leftovers can be refrigerated
> and warmed in the microwave. The
> noodles will get soft and chewy again.

1   While you cut the vegetables, soak the noodles in warm water until they're pliable, about 10 minutes. Drain and cut into shorter lengths with kitchen shears so the strands fit in your Instant Pot®.

2   Select SAUTÉ and set to NORMAL/MEDIUM. Add the oil. When the pot is hot, add the garlic and onion and stir and cook until fragrant, about 30 seconds. Add the carrots and mushrooms followed by the soy sauce, sugar and sesame oil. Stir to mix. Press CANCEL.

3   Pour in the chicken stock and stir, scraping the bottom of the pot to remove any cooked-on bits to avoid the BURN warning. Add the noodles and press down to submerge as much as possible.

4   Lock the lid. Select PRESSURE COOK/MANUAL and set to HIGH for 3 minutes. Make sure the steam release valve is sealed. Once pressurized (9 to 11 minutes), the cook cycle will start. When the timer beeps, manually release the pressure. When the float valve drops, press CANCEL and open the lid.

5   Select SAUTÉ and set to NORMAL/MEDIUM. Stir in the green onions and spinach and toss to coat the noodles and vegetables evenly in sauce. If the noodles look dry, and/or are sticking to the pot, add a little more stock or water to loosen. Taste, and add salt, pepper and other seasonings as desired. Press CANCEL.

6   Sprinkle with sesame seeds and serve with rice and a meat dish like Marinated Pork Bulgogi (page 102) or Braised Korean Short Ribs (page 81). You can also use it top Korean Bibimbap Mixed Rice Bowl (page 64).

Chicken Lo Mein

You can usually find wheat noodles labeled "lo mein" at the grocery store. If you can't find them, my recipe tester Kay has a brilliant idea: look for Asian wheat or egg noodles that have a similar cook time of 5 to 6 minutes. Or use linguine and cook for 8 minutes on HIGH.

PREP TIME: 10 minutes **TOTAL TIME:** 30 minutes
MAKES: 4 servings

2 boneless, skinless chicken thighs or breasts (¾ to 1 pound/450 g), cut into 1-inch (2.5-cm) pieces
4 tablespoons oyster sauce, divided
2 tablespoons vegetable oil
2 teaspoons minced garlic
1 teaspoon minced fresh ginger
½ cup (60 g) sliced onion
2 tablespoons soy sauce
2 teaspoons sesame oil
1 teaspoon sugar
8 ounces (200 g) dried lo mein noodles
2¼ cups (540 ml) low-sodium chicken stock or water
1 cup (60 g) sliced fresh mushrooms such as button, shiitake or cremini
½ cup (60 g) carrot cut in matchsticks
1 cup (120 g) snow peas, halved
2 cups (345 g) loosely packed baby spinach or chopped spinach
Fine sea salt and freshly ground pepper to taste
Chopped green onions, for garnish

> **NOTES:** Hoisin sauce or dark soy sauce is a great substitute for oyster sauce in this recipe.

1 Mix the chicken with 1 tablespoon oyster sauce.

2 Select SAUTÉ and set to MEDIUM/NORMAL. Add the oil. When the pot is hot, add the garlic, ginger and onion and stir and cook until fragrant, about 30 seconds. Add the chicken and stir and cook until seared on all sides, 3 to 5 minutes. Press CANCEL.

3 Stir in the remaining 3 tablespoons oyster sauce, soy sauce, sesame oil and sugar. Add the noodles, breaking them if necessary, and pour in the stock. Bathe the noodles in sauce. Place the mushrooms on top.

4 Lock the lid. Select PRESSURE COOK/MANUAL and set to HIGH for 5 minutes. Make sure the steam release valve is sealed. Once pressurized (9 to 12 minutes),

the cook cycle will start. When the timer beeps, manually release the pressure. When the float valve drops, press CANCEL and open the lid. The noodles will not be fully cooked yet, and there will be excess sauce.

5 Select SAUTÉ and set to MEDIUM/NORMAL. Stir in the carrots and snow peas with a wooden spoon. Season with salt and pepper to taste. Keep stirring and separate any noodles that have clumped together. When the noodles are almost done, about 3 minutes, add the spinach and continue to stir. After 1 to 2 minutes, the noodles will be fully cooked and the sauce evaporated. Add more stock or water, if the noodles start to stick to the pot.

6 Sprinkle with green onions and serve.

Thai Basil Chicken Rice

This dish is a riff on *pad grapow moo*, the very popular Thai basil pork dish. Use chicken breast if you'd like, but I suggest using whole breasts and then cutting them up at the end to prevent the meat from getting too dry. Ground pork or turkey is also tasty.

PREP TIME: 10 minutes **TOTAL TIME:** 30 minutes
MAKES: 4 servings

3 tablespoons soy sauce
2 tablespoons fish sauce
¼ cup (60 ml) Thai sweet chili sauce
1 teaspoon chili paste like *sambal oelek*
1 tablespoon vegetable oil
2 tablespoons minced garlic (6 medium cloves)
½ cup sliced shallots (1 medium)
1 pound (450 g) boneless, skinless chicken thighs, cut into ¾- to 1-inch (2- to 2.5-cm) cubes (about 2 to 3 thighs)
1½ cups (300 g) uncooked jasmine rice, rinsed until the water runs clear, and drained
1½ cups (360 ml) low-sodium chicken stock
1 cup (130 g) frozen green peas (or other quick-cooking vegetable like spinach or snow peas)
1½ cups loosely packed Thai basil leaves, torn if large
Freshly ground black pepper

NOTES: For a sweet chili sauce substitute, pair a teaspoon of chili paste/sauce with a tablespoon of honey or plum sauce, then adjust to your liking. Opt for a sauce with a minimal amount of vinegar like sriracha or *sambal oelek*.

My recipe tester Marcie suggested squeezing lime juice over the dish for some brightness.

1 Mix together the soy sauce, fish sauce, sweet chili sauce and chili paste in a small bowl.
2 Select SAUTÉ and set to NORMAL/MEDIUM. Add the vegetable oil. When the pot is hot, add the garlic and shallot and stir and cook until fragrant, about 30 seconds.
3 Add the chicken and sear on all sides until barely any pink is left, 2 to 3 minutes. Press CANCEL.
4 Pour in the sauce and scrape the bottom of the pot to remove any cooked-on bits and avoid the BURN warning. Stir in the rice and coat evenly with the sauce. Pour in the stock and stir to mix.
5 Lock the lid. Select PRESSURE COOK/MANUAL and set to HIGH for 4 minutes.

Make sure the steam release valve is sealed. Once pressurized (8 to 12 minutes), the cook cycle will start. When the timer beeps, let the pressure release naturally for 5 minutes. Then quick release any remaining pressure. When the float valve drops, press CANCEL and open the lid.
6 Select SAUTÉ and set to NORMAL/MEDIUM. Stir the green peas into the rice for about 1 minute. Gently fold in the Thai basil and stir and cook until the peas turn bright green, the basil wilts and all the sauce has evaporated.
7 Taste and adjust seasonings if desired. Divide among 4 plates or bowls and grind pepper over and serve.

Filipino Pancit Canton Noodles with Pork

Pancit Canton is a Filipino noodle dish made with Chinese wheat noodles usually seasoned with *toyomansi*, a Filipino soy sauce flavored with Asian limes called *calamansi*. I just use a combo of soy sauce and lemon/lime juice. If you can find *calamansi* at the Asian market, either fresh or frozen in little packets, use it! It's what makes this dish special.

PREP TIME: 10 minutes **TOTAL TIME:** 30 minutes
MAKES: 4 to 6 servings

6 ounces (180 g) pork shoulder or loin, sliced into bite-sized pieces

1 teaspoon plus 3 tablespoons soy sauce

1 teaspoon plus 2 tablespoons lemon or lime juice

1 tablespoon vegetable oil

1 tablespoon minced garlic (3 medium cloves)

1½ cups (200 g) sliced onion

3 cups cabbage chopped into 2-inch (5-cm) squares

2 large carrots, peeled and chopped into 1-inch-thick (2.5-cm) rounds (2 cups)

1 teaspoon sugar

½ teaspoon salt

¼ teaspoon freshly ground black pepper

8 ounces (200 g) dried *pancit canton* or other Chinese wheat noodles

2¼ cups (540 ml) low-sodium chicken stock or water

1 cup green onions cut into 1-inch (2.5-cm) segments

NOTES: Note that different brands of noodles have different cooking times and use different amounts of stock. So you might have to adjust.

I like to add Chinese sausage (page 76) to this dish too, but feel free to use chicken, shrimp or beef, or make it vegetarian!

The vegetables will be a little softer than usual after cooking in the pressure cooker for 5 minutes. If you prefer your vegetables crisp-tender, cut them into matchsticks. Select SAUTÉ and set to HIGH/MORE and stir the vegetables in with the green onions. Or, you can steam or microwave the vegetables in bite-sized pieces and add them right at the very end.

1   Marinate the pork with 1 teaspoon soy sauce and 1 teaspoon lemon juice.

2   Select SAUTÉ and set to HIGH/MORE. Add the vegetable oil. When the pot is hot, add the garlic and onion and stir and cook until fragrant and the onion has softened, 1 to 1½ minutes. Move the aromatics to one side. Add the pork and sear on all sides until barely pink, 1 to 2 minutes. Mix everything together. Add the cabbage and carrots one after the other, stirring for about 30 seconds in between. Press CANCEL.

3   Add the remaining soy sauce and lemon juice, sugar, salt and pepper and mix well, scraping the bottom of the pot to remove any cooked-on bits and avoid the BURN warning. Add the noodles, breaking them up if necessary to fit inside the pot. Pour in the stock and push down to make sure the noodles are below the maximum fill line.

4   Lock the lid. Select PRESSURE COOK/MANUAL and set to HIGH for 5 minutes. Make sure the steam release valve is sealed. Once pressurized (10 to 12 minutes), the cook cycle will start. When the timer beeps, manually release the pressure. When the float valve drops, press CANCEL and open the lid. At this point, the noodles will be a little undercooked and there will be excess sauce.

5   Select SAUTÉ and set to MEDIUM/NORMAL. Add the green onions and continue stirring until some—but not all!—the sauce has evaporated and the noodles are fully cooked, 1 to 2 minutes. Keep in mind the noodles should be a little saucy. Press CANCEL.

6   Scoop the noodles onto a serving plate and serve hot with lemon wedges.

Pad Thai

The key to this recipe is using the right kind of noodles. Pick a noodle about the width of linguine. Err on the side of wider noodles. Noodles that are too skinny will become mushy. I also believe that the drop lid makes all the difference—it allows the noodles to cook evenly without too much liquid, which can turn them soggy. My recipe tester Laura loves that this pad Thai recipe doesn't turn out as greasy as some restaurant versions do.

PREP TIME: 15 minutes (not including tamarind preparation) **TOTAL TIME:** 35 minutes
MAKES: 4 servings

8 ounces (225 g) dried rice noodles, size: M (⅛ inch or 3 mm), broken up if necessary
6 ounces (180 g) boneless, skinless chicken thigh or breast, sliced thinly
Vegetable oil, divided
3 large eggs, beaten
1 tablespoon minced garlic, (3 medium cloves)
½ cup chopped shallot (1 small)
2 tablespoons dried shrimp, chopped (optional)
2 tablespoons chopped sweetened preserved radish
1¼ cups (300 ml) low-sodium chicken stock, divided
4 ounces (120 g) baked tofu cut into 1-inch-long x ½-inch-wide x ¼-inch-thick (2.5 cm x 1.25 cm x 6 mm) sticks
½ cup green onions chopped into 2-inch (5-cm) lengths

SAUCE
3 tablespoons coconut sugar or 2 tablespoons brown sugar
2 tablespoons granulated sugar
3 tablespoons tamarind extract (page 18) or white vinegar
3 to 4 tablespoons fish sauce, plus more to marinate the chicken

GARNISHES
1 cup (100 g) bean sprouts
1 cup shredded carrots (50 g)
¼ cup (30 g) crushed roasted peanuts (optional)
2 tablespoons dry roasted chilies (optional)
1 lime, cut into wedges

SPECIAL EQUIPMENT
Drop lid (page 11)

1 Make the sauce. Simmer the coconut and granulated sugars, tamarind extract and fish sauce in a small saucepan over medium heat until the sugars are completely dissolved, about 1 minute. Or microwave in a heatproof bowl on MEDIUM for 1 minute.

2 Soak the noodles in lukewarm tap water for 10 minutes. Drain.

3 Marinate the chicken with a few dashes of fish sauce.

4 Select SAUTÉ and adjust to HIGH/MORE. Add 1 tablespoon vegetable oil. When the pot is hot, add the chicken and sear on all sides until barely any pink remains, 1 to 2 minutes. Add 1 more teaspoon oil if the pot looks dry. Pour the eggs over the chicken and let sit until just set, 30 seconds to 1 minute. Mix everything together and scramble the eggs briefly into large curds. Remove while the egg is still "wet." (See Notes)

5 Add 2 teaspoons oil. Scrape the pot to remove any stuck-on egg. Add the garlic, shallot, dried shrimp and preserved radish, stir-frying a few times between each addition. Cook and stir until fragrant, 1 to 2 minutes. Press CANCEL.

6 Add about ¼ cup (60 ml) stock to the pot and scrape the bottom to remove any cooked-on bits and avoid the BURN warning. Stir in the remaining 1 cup stock and the sauce. Add the noodles and bathe in the sauce. Don't worry if the noodles aren't submerged. Place the drop lid on top to promote even cooking.

7 Lock the lid. Select PRESSURE COOK/MANUAL and set to LOW for 1 minutes. Make sure the steam release valve is sealed. Once pressurized (5 to 7 minutes), the cook cycle will start. When the timer beeps, manually release the pressure. When the float valve drops, press CANCEL and open the lid. The noodles will be soft but still pale on top.

8 Select SAUTÉ and set to MEDIUM/NORMAL. Keep stirring with a wooden spoon to distribute the sauce, and loosen and separate the noodles. If the noodles are not tender enough to your liking, add stock or water a little at a time and keep stirring. Add the green onions and stir until slightly wilted, about 1 minute. Add the chicken, egg and baked tofu, and stir and cook until warmed through. Taste. Add fish sauce to make it saltier, or sugar for extra sweetness. Press CANCEL.

9 Divide among 4 plates. Top with bean sprouts and/or carrots. Serve immediately with garnishes in small dishes.

> **NOTES:** Both dried shrimp and preserved radish are important components of making traditional pad Thai. But if you can't find them or don't want to use them, the pad Thai police won't come after you.
>   You can use fresh peeled shrimp instead of, or in addition to, the chicken, and add it to the noodles at the end.
>   Baked tofu is sold in the refrigerated section at both mainstream grocery stores and Asian markets. It's already cooked so all you need to do is heat it up with the noodles.

NOTES: I designed this as a one-pot recipe, but you'll have to diligently scrape off stuck-on egg. You can also cook the chicken and egg in a nonstick pan on the stove. This will also lower your chances of getting a BURN warning from the newer Instant Pot® models.

I like my pad Thai noodles al dente. Add more water and/or cook longer if you like your noodles softer.

If tamarind isn't available, you can use white vinegar instead. While also sour, white vinegar has a different character from tamarind, and the flavor won't be as complex. Feel free to adjust the amount as desired.

NOTES: I like to use the tomato sauce jar to measure out the water. I'll fill the jar with water and shake to dislodge the remaining sauce. Not a single bit is wasted! 4 cups = 1½ (24-ounce) jars = 32 ounces.

Tomato sauce is basically tomatoes blitzed in a blender and strained of skin and seeds. It's also called passata. It's not the same as tomato ketchup, but you can use regular pasta sauce if that's all you can find.

Filipino-Style Spaghetti

Filipino spaghetti recipes tend to be sweet-sweet-sweet! This sweetness is accentuated by banana ketchup, a very Filipino condiment invented during World War II when tomatoes were scarce. You can order it online or make your own by mashing half a banana into a puree and mixing it with ¾ cup (180 ml) tomato ketchup (I have cookbook author Marvin Gapultos's blessing). Or just use regular tomato ketchup.

PREP TIME: 10 minutes TOTAL TIME: 45 minutes
MAKES: 4 to 6 servings

3 tablespoons olive oil
2 tablespoons chopped garlic (6 medium cloves)
2 cups (360 g) chopped onion
½ cup chopped carrot
½ cup chopped red bell pepper
1 pound (450 g) ground pork or Italian sausage
4 hot dogs (400 g), sliced (about 2 cups)
6 tablespoons double-concentrate tomato paste (or a 6-ounce/180-g can)
4 cups (960 ml) water, divided
1 (24-ounce/710-ml) jar tomato sauce (3 cups/720 ml)
1 cup (240 ml) banana ketchup
1 tablespoon granulated sugar
1 teaspoon fine sea salt
Freshly ground black pepper to taste
1 (1-pound/450-g) box spaghetti
1 cup (115 g) shredded cheddar cheese (or any cheese that melts)

1 Select SAUTÉ and set to HIGH/MORE. Add the oil. When the pot is hot, add the garlic, onion, carrots and bell pepper and stir and cook until fragrant, 1 to 2 minutes. Add the pork and brown for 1 to 2 minutes. Add the hot dogs and stir and cook until the pork is barely pink, 2 to 3 more minutes. Add the tomato paste and mix to coat the meat and vegetables. Press CANCEL.
2 Pour 1 cup (240 ml) water into the pot and scrape the bottom of the pot to remove any cooked-on bits and avoid the BURN warning.
3 Add the tomato sauce, banana ketchup and 3 cups (720 ml) water, scraping as you go. Add the sugar, salt and pepper and stir to mix.
4 Make a shallow well in the middle of the sauce. Take small bunches of spaghetti and break the noodles in half. Place the noodles in the well and cover with sauce as best as you can. Make sure there is sauce both under and over the noodles for even cooking. Don't stir to prevent clumping.
5 Lock the lid. Select PRESSURE COOK/MANUAL and set to HIGH for 8 minutes. Make sure the steam release valve is sealed. Once pressurized (18 to 20 minutes), the cook cycle will start. When the timer beeps, manually release the pressure. When the float valve drops, press CANCEL and open the lid.
6 Select SAUTÉ and set to MEDIUM/NORMAL. Stir the noodles until they are cooked to your liking and the remaining sauce clings to the noodles, 2 to 3 minutes.
7 Scoop into individual pasta bowls and pass the cheese at the table.

HOW TO MAKE FILIPINO SPAGHETTI

Fried Rice "Risotto"

You might be wondering what the heck is fried rice risotto? Well, it's just risotto made with ingredients I normally throw into fried rice. I left out the cheese, but I couldn't resist adding butter. The richness of full-cream butter paired with oyster sauce and soy sauces is divine!

PREP TIME: 15 minutes TOTAL TIME: 40 minutes
MAKES: 4 to 6 servings

1 teaspoon vegetable oil
4 Chinese sausage links, cut into
¼-inch (6.25-mm) slices
3 tablespoons unsalted butter, divided
1 tablespoon minced garlic (3 medium
cloves)
1 tablespoon minced fresh ginger
½ cup (120 g) minced shallot
1½ cups (320 g) short-grain Japanese-
Style rice, rinsed in 2 to 3 changes of
water and drained
3 tablespoons Chinese cooking wine
2 tablespoons oyster sauce
1 tablespoon soy sauce
3½ cups (840 ml) low-sodium chicken
stock, plus more as needed
8 ounces (200 g) bok choy or Chinese
cabbage, sliced into thin ribbons,
stalks and leaves kept separate
1 cup (130 g) frozen peas and/or carrots
2 teaspoons rice vinegar
2 teaspoons sesame oil
¼ teaspoon freshly ground black
pepper
Fine sea salt, to taste
Cilantro/coriander leaves, to garnish

SPECIAL EQUIPMENT
Paper towels
Plate

1 Select SAUTÉ and set to HIGH/MORE. Add the vegetable oil. When the pot is hot, add the Chinese sausage and cook until browned on all sides, 3 to 4 minutes. Remove to a plate lined with paper towels. Drain the fat if desired.

2 Melt 1 tablespoon butter in the pot and add the garlic, ginger and shallot. Cook and stir until the shallot has softened, 2 to 3 minutes.

3 Add the rice and stir continuously, for 1 minute. Add the cooking wine, oyster sauce and soy sauce and stir to coat. Press CANCEL.

4 Pour in 3½ cups (840 ml) stock and stir, scraping the bottom of the pot to remove any cooked-on bits and avoid the BURN warning.

5 Lock the lid. Select PRESSURE COOK/MANUAL and set to HIGH for 8 minutes.

Make sure the steam release valve is sealed. Once pressurized (9 to 11 minutes), the cook cycle will start. When the timer beeps, manually release the pressure. When the float valve drops, press CANCEL and open the lid.

6 Select SAUTÉ and set to MEDIUM/NORMAL. Add the bok choy stems and stir for 30 seconds. Then add the bok choy leaves, peas and carrots. Stir and cook until the vegetables are crisp-tender, about 2 more minutes. Add ½ to 1 cup (120 to 240 ml) more stock while cooking, to keep the risotto saucy.

7 Stir in the remaining 2 tablespoons butter, rice vinegar and sesame oil. Season with pepper and salt to taste. Fold the Chinese sausage into the risotto. Press CANCEL. Garnish with cilantro/coriander leaves and serve.

> **NOTES:** Chinese sausages are known as *lop cheung* in Cantonese. Made of ground pork and pork fat, they are cured but not cooked. You can find them packaged in cellophane at Asian markets. Refrigerate for 3 months or freeze for up to 6.
>
> No Chinese sausages? Use store-bought Chinese barbecued pork or leftover rotisserie chicken instead. Even ham would be tasty!

Vietnamese Garlic Butter Noodles

When I lived in Northern California, I heard rumors about the famous recipes prepared in the secret kitchen of the An family's Vietnamese restaurant, Thanh Long. One of these famed recipes was garlic butter noodles, often served with their also legendary roasted garlic crab. I never ate there, but this is my rendition that I've conjured based on info culled from the blogosphere.

PREP TIME: 5 minutes **TOTAL TIME:** 20 minutes
MAKES: 4 servings to accompany an entree

4 tablespoons butter, divided
2 tablespoons minced garlic (6 medium cloves)
2 green onions, chopped green and white parts separated, plus more for garnish
2 tablespoons oyster sauce
1 tablespoon soy sauce
1 tablespoon fish sauce
1 tablespoon light brown sugar
2 cups (480 ml) low-sodium chicken stock
8 ounces (200 g) dried Chinese egg noodles or spaghetti
Fried garlic bits (see Notes)
2 tablespoons grated Parmesan cheese (optional)

1 Select SAUTÉ and set to HIGH/MORE. Add 1 tablespoon butter. When the pot is hot and the butter has melted, add the garlic and white portions of the green onions. Stir and cook until fragrant, about 30 seconds. Press CANCEL.

2 Add the oyster, soy and fish sauces, sugar and stock. Stir to mix, scraping the bottom of the pot to remove any cooked-on bits and avoid the BURN warning.

3 Add the noodles, breaking them if necessary to get them below the maximum fill line. Bathe the noodles in the sauce.

4 Lock the lid. Select PRESSURE COOK/MANUAL and set to HIGH for 4 minutes (6 minutes for spaghetti). Make sure the steam release valve is sealed. Once pressurized (6 to 8 minutes), the cook cycle will start. When the timer beeps, manually release the pressure. When the float valve drops, press CANCEL and open the lid.

5 There will be excess sauce, but it will evaporate as you stir the noodles.

6 Select SAUTÉ and set to MEDIUM/NORMAL. Add 3 tablespoons butter cut into small pieces and the rest of the green onions. Toss with a pair of tongs, separating any noodles that are stuck together, until the butter has melted and mixed into the noodles, 2 to 3 minutes.

7 Divide among 4 plates and sprinkle with more green onions, fried garlic bits and cheese, if using.

> **NOTES:** To make this a complete meal, stir in some quick-cooking vegetables like peas, chopped spinach or snow peas together with the butter and green onions. Top with leftover meat.

> **NOTES:** To make your own fried garlic bits, mince 3 to 4 garlic cloves and place in a large microwave-safe bowl with 2 tablespoons of vegetable oil. Microwave on medium for 30 seconds at a time until the garlic turns golden brown. Depending on your microwave, this could take up to 2 minutes. Keep in mind that it will continue to cook in the hot oil after it is taken out of the microwave. Strain and use the garlic bits as garnish, and keep the oil for another use.

Beef Dishes

In Asian cooking, beef is often cooked with vegetables and served with rice. Thankfully, the Instant Pot® speeds the process for notoriously long-cooking cuts like short ribs and oxtails.

Japanese-Style Beef and Potato Stew · Nikujaga

Niku in Japanese means "meat." *Jaga* is short for *jagaimo*, which means "potatoes" in Japanese. So *Nikujaga* always includes meat and potatoes. Japanese recipes like this one, combining meat and vegetables, are ideal for pressure cooking. Since it uses thinly sliced meat, both the meat and the vegetables will cook at roughly the same time.

PREP TIME: 10 minutes **TOTAL TIME:** 55 minutes
MAKES: 4 servings

8 ounces (200 g) sirloin tip, tenderloin, or skirt steak
1 cup (240 ml) Dashi (page 23) or low-sodium beef or chicken stock
3 tablespoons soy sauce
1 tablespoon mirin
1 tablespoon granulated sugar
1 medium onion cut into 8 wedges and separated (8 ounces/200 g)
2 medium (¾ pound/360 g) yellow gold or russet potatoes, peeled and cut into quarters
2 large carrots (6 ounces/180 g), peeled and chopped into 1-inch-thick (2.5-cm) pieces
1 cup (150 g) snow peas, trimmed and halved if large

1 Slice the beef into ⅛-inch-thick (3-mm) slices. (see page 83 for tips).
2 Stir together the dashi, soy sauce, mirin and sugar in the pot. Add the beef, onion, potatoes and carrots and stir to coat evenly with sauce. Place a drop lid (page 11) on top.
3 Lock the lid. Select PRESSURE COOK/MANUAL and set to HIGH for 12 minutes. Make sure the steam release valve is sealed. Once pressurized (15 to 20 minutes), the cook cycle will start. When the timer beeps, let the pressure release naturally for 15 minutes. Then quick release any remaining pressure. When the float valve drops, press CANCEL and open the lid.
4 Stir in the snow peas and cook in the residual heat for about 30 seconds. Serve with steamed white rice.

> **NOTES:** Skirt steak, sirloin tip or tenderloin all have a similar loose grain that holds marinade well and, when cooked, has a chewy but not tough consistency.

Braised Korean Short Ribs   Kalbijjim

This hearty Korean dish can be made with beef or pork short ribs. Using the Instant Pot® makes quick work of this normally slow-cooked dish. Leaving out the parboiling and searing steps doesn't sacrifice any flavor, but if you don't like it too oily, you might want to parboil the meat first.

PREP TIME: 10 minutes **TOTAL TIME:** 1 hour, 15 minutes **MAKES:** 4 to 6 servings

2 pounds (900 g) beef short ribs
1 kiwi or half an Asian pear, peeled and pureed as a meat tenderizer
1 tablespoon light brown sugar
1 cup (120 g) sliced onion
2 large carrots (1 pound/450 g), cut into 1½-inch-thick (3.75-cm) pieces
8 ounces (240 g) daikon radish, peeled and cut into large 1½-inch-thick (3.75-cm) pieces
8 rehydrated (page 13) black mushrooms (2 ounces/60 g)

SAUCE
¼ cup (60 ml) soy sauce
1 tablespoon Chinese cooking wine
2 tablespoons minced garlic (6 medium cloves)
1 tablespoon grated fresh ginger
2 teaspoons gochugaru, or to taste
¼ teaspoon freshly ground black pepper

TO FINISH
1 tablespoon maple syrup or honey
1 tablespoon sesame oil
Chopped green onions
Toasted sesame seeds

> **NOTES:** My recipe tester Naomi suggests using top blade steaks or pot roast cut into hunks.
> Gochugaru is available both coarsely and finely ground. Either works for this recipe. You can certainly use cayenne, but use it sparingly because it's much spicier.

1 Trim the short ribs of extra fat. Massage them with the kiwi puree and brown sugar.
2 Place the short ribs, onion, carrot, daikon and mushrooms in the pot. Pour the sauce over and stir to mix well. During cooking, the meat and vegetables will release their juices so you don't need to add more water.
3 Make the sauce. Whisk together the soy sauce, cooking wine, garlic, ginger, gochugaru and black pepper in a measuring cup. You'll have ⅓ about cup (80 ml).
4 Lock the lid. Select PRESSURE COOK/MANUAL and set to HIGH for 35 minutes. Make sure the steam release valve is sealed. Once pressurized (15 to 20 minutes), the cook cycle will start. When the

timer beeps, let the pressure release naturally for 15 minutes. Then quick release any remaining pressure. When the float valve drops, press CANCEL and open the lid.
5 Remove the meat and vegetables from the pot and skim off the fat. If you're not going to eat immediately, you can refrigerate the sauce until the fat solidifies on top, making it easier to remove. Then reheat and/or reduce the sauce.
6 To reduce the sauce, select SAUTÉ and set to HIGH/MORE. Simmer for 5 to 10 minutes or until desired consistency. Stir in the maple syrup and sesame oil.
7 Pour the sauce over the ribs, and garnish with the green onions and sesame seeds. Serve with steamed rice.

NOTES: My recipe tester Betty Ann has these tips: Before marinating the meat, pound the fillets with a mallet to tenderize the meat further. You can make this with pork tenderloin as well.

Tangy Filipino Beefsteak

This supereasy Filipino dish is defined by a citrus called *calamansi*. Although widespread in Southeast Asia, *calamansi* is hard to find in North America. It's usually available as a frozen concentrate at Asian markets and even fresh in California. Meyer lemon closely mimics *calamansi's* sweet-tart floral flavor and is my first choice as a replacement. Both *calamansi* and Meyer lemon are less sour than regular lemons, so use a combo of lemon and orange juice if you cannot find those.

PREP TIME: 10 minutes **TOTAL TIME:** 45 minutes plus marinating time **MAKES:** 4 to 6 servings

1 pound (450 g) flank steak, sirloin or skirt steak, cut into ⅛-inch-thick (3-mm) slices
3 tablespoons vegetable oil, divided
1 medium onion, sliced into thin rings (1½ cups/240 g)
Fine sea salt

MARINADE
½ cup (120 ml) *calamansi* or Meyer lemon juice, or ¼ cup (60 ml) lemon juice plus ¼ cup (60 ml) orange juice
2 tablespoons soy sauce
1 tablespoon minced garlic, (3 medium cloves)
½ teaspoon freshly ground black pepper, plus more as needed

NOTES: If the sauce is too sour, which can happen if you use only regular lemon juice, add 1 to 2 teaspoons brown sugar while reducing the sauce.

1 Toss the beef with the marinade: *calamansi* juice, soy sauce, garlic and pepper. Cover and marinate in the refrigerator for at least an hour.
2 Drain the beef and blot dry with paper towels. Reserve the marinade.
3 Select SAUTÉ and set to HIGH/MORE. Add 2 tablespoons oil. When the pot is hot, add the onion and sprinkle with salt and pepper to taste. Stir and cook until softened and lightly caramelized, 3 to 4 minutes. Remove with tongs.
4 Add 1 more tablespoon of oil. When the pot is hot, add the beef and sear 1 to 2 minutes on each side. Pour in the marinade and scrape the bottom of the pot to remove any cooked-on bits and avoid the BURN warning.
5 Lock the lid. Select PRESSURE COOK/

MANUAL and set to HIGH for 10 minutes. Make sure the steam release valve is sealed. Once pressurized (8 to 12 minutes), the cook cycle will start.
6 When the timer beeps, let the pressure release naturally for 10 minutes. Then quick release any remaining pressure. When the float valve drops, press CANCEL and open the lid.
7 Remove the beef to a serving plate with a slotted spoon. Place the onions on top. Tent with foil to keep warm.
8 Select SAUTÉ and set to HIGH/MORE to reduce the sauce to your liking. Taste and adjust seasonings if desired. Once the sauce is ready, press CANCEL. Pour the sauce over the steak and onions.
9 Serve with steamed rice and a vegetable side dish.

HOW TO CUT THE MEAT

1. Handle the meat while partially frozen (30 minutes in the freezer should do it) to make it easier to slice.
2. Trim large pieces of membrane.
3. Find the direction of the grain (the way the muscle fibers are aligned). Cut along the grain into 2- to 3-inch-wide (5- to 7.5-cm) strips.
4. With your knife almost parallel to the cutting board, slice across the grain into ⅛-inch-thick (3-mm) slices. Assuming your piece of meat is about 1 inch (2.5 cm) thick, you'll end up with strips 2 inches (7.5 cm) long, 1 inch (2.5 cm) wide and ⅛ inch (3 mm) thick.

Beef with Broccoli

The Mongolian beef or beef and broccoli served at Chinese restaurants in the U.S. tends to be too sweet for my taste. I've developed a more authentic version, easy on the sugar, and very tasty. As with many traditional Asian dishes, the meat is minimal, but feel free to increase the amount of beef (or sugar for that matter!).

PPREP TIME: 10 minutes **TOTAL TIME:** 40 minutes
MAKES: 4 servings

1 pound (450 g) flank steak, sirloin or top round beef, cut into ⅛-inch-thick (3-mm) slices (see pg 83)
2 tablespoons vegetable oil, plus more as needed
1 tablespoon minced garlic (3 medium cloves)
1 tablespoon grated fresh ginger
2 cups (360 g) broccoli florets

MARINADE
1 tablespoon soy sauce
1 tablespoon sesame oil
1 tablespoon Chinese cooking wine
1 tablespoon cornstarch
¼ teaspoon fine sea salt
¼ teaspoon granulated sugar

SAUCE
2 tablespoons soy sauce
1 tablespoon rice vinegar
1 tablespoon sesame oil
1 teaspoon chili paste (optional)
2 to 3 tablespoons brown sugar
¼ cup (60 ml) plus 2 tablespoons low-sodium chicken stock

TO FINISH
2 teaspoons cornstarch mixed with 2 tablespoons water to make a slurry (optional)
Toasted sesame seeds, to garnish

1 Toss the beef with the marinade: soy sauce, sesame oil, cooking wine, cornstarch, salt and sugar. Set aside (you can do this ahead and refrigerate for several hours).

2 Make the sauce. Whisk together the soy sauce, vinegar, sesame oil, chili paste (if using), brown sugar and stock in a separate bowl.

3 Select SAUTÉ and set to HIGH/MORE. Add 2 tablespoons vegetable oil. When the pot is hot, add the beef and sear on all sides for about 2 minutes. Don't worry if it's not fully cooked.

4 Add more oil to the pot if it looks dry. Add the garlic and ginger. Stir and cook until fragrant, about 30 seconds. Press CANCEL.

5 Gradually pour in the sauce, scraping the bottom of the pot to remove any cooked-on bits and avoid the BURN warning.

6 Lock the lid. Select PRESSURE COOK/MANUAL and set to HIGH for 10 minutes. Make sure the steam release valve is sealed. Once pressurized (7 to 11 minutes), the cook cycle will start.

7 While the beef is cooking, microwave the broccoli, covered, in a heatproof bowl with ¼ cup (60 ml) water for 2 to 3 minutes until crisp tender.

8 When the timer beeps, let the pressure release naturally for 10 minutes. Then quick release any remaining pressure. When the float valve drops, press CANCEL and open the lid.

9 Transfer the beef with a slotted spoon to a serving plate. Tent with foil to keep warm.

10 If you'd like to thicken the sauce, select SAUTÉ and set to MEDIUM/NORMAL. Stir in the cornstarch slurry a little at a time until the sauce thickens to desired consistency. Keep in mind that the sauce will continue to thicken as it cools. Taste and adjust seasonings if desired. Stir in the cooked broccoli.

11 Press CANCEL and pour the broccoli and sauce over the beef. Garnish with sesame seeds and serve immediately with steamed rice.

> **NOTES:** For convenience, buy frozen broccoli that can be steamed directly in the bag in the microwave.
> If you don't have a microwave oven, cook the broccoli directly in the Instant Pot®. On SAUTÉ, before you add the cornstarch to thicken the sauce, add the broccoli. Cover and cook for 2 to 3 minutes.

Chicken Dishes

Traditionally, Asian-Style chicken is cooked whole or bone-in, and dark meat is preferred. In the Instant Pot®, curries and braises are cooked until the meat is fall-off-the-bone tender.

Lemon Teriyaki Glazed Chicken

Teriyaki chicken is brightened up with some lemon juice for a sweet-tart take on this Japanese favorite. Chicken thighs are tastiest, but swap them out for chicken breasts if you prefer. Find small thighs to fit in one layer in the 6-quart Instant Pot®.

PREP TIME: 5 minutes TOTAL TIME: 33 minutes
MAKES: 4 servings

3 tablespoons granulated sugar
3 tablespoons brown sugar
1 tablespoon minced garlic (3 medium cloves)
1 teaspoon grated fresh ginger
½ cup (120 ml) soy sauce
¼ cup (60 ml) fresh lemon juice (1 large lemon)
6 small bone-in, skin-on chicken thighs (about 2 pounds/900 g)
3 medium carrots, peeled and sliced thinly (1 cup)
2 cups (300 g) snow peas, trimmed and halved if large

1 Whisk together the granulated and brown sugars, garlic, ginger, soy sauce and lemon juice in the pot. Coat both sides of the chicken in the sauce and nestle skin side up in one layer. It might be a tight fit, but you can do it!

2 Lock the lid. Select PRESSURE COOK/MANUAL and set to HIGH for 9 minutes. Make sure the steam release valve is sealed. Once pressurized (10 to 15 minutes), the cook cycle will start.

3 When the timer beeps, let the pressure release naturally for 5 minutes. Then quick release any remaining pressure. When the float valve drops, press CANCEL and open the lid.

4 Transfer the chicken with a slotted spoon or tongs to a serving dish and tent with foil. Skim the fat from the sauce.

5 Select SAUTÉ and set to HIGH/MORE. Add the carrots and cook until crisp-tender, 4 to 5 minutes. Stir in the snow peas and let sit 30 seconds. Press CANCEL.

6 Pour the sauce and vegetables over the chicken and serve with steamed rice.

> **NOTES:** Feel free to use any quick-cooking vegetable at the end.
>   My recipe tester Pat offered this tip: Keep the skin on the chicken when cooking. The skin gets a little flabby after cooking but helps keep the chicken from drying out!

NOTES: Guide to chicken thigh cooking times:
Bone-in, skin-on: 9 minutes
Boneless, skinless: 7 minutes
Frozen (either bone-in or boneless): 11 minutes

Orange Chicken

Orange Chicken is just a variation on another Chinese crowd pleaser, General Tso's Chicken. Unlike the thick-battered pieces of chicken doused in a sticky sweet sauce you might be used to, my version is much lighter and doesn't involve any deep-frying but has all the flavor of the restaurant versions. Orange beef is a popular variation—simply substitute flank steak or sirloin tips for the chicken.

PREP TIME: 10 minutes COOK: 20 minutes TOTAL TIME: 30 minutes MAKES: 4 servings

1 pound (450 g) boneless, skinless chicken thighs cut into 1½-inch (7.5-cm) cubes
1 tablespoon fresh orange juice
1 tablespoon soy sauce
2 teaspoons Chinese rice cooking wine

SAUCE
¼ cup (60 ml) fresh orange juice (1 large orange)
2 tablespoons soy sauce
1 tablespoon Chinese rice cooking wine
1 teaspoon sesame oil
1 teaspoon rice vinegar
2 teaspoons granulated sugar

1 tablespoon vegetable oil
2 teaspoons minced garlic (2 medium cloves)
2 teaspoons minced fresh ginger
5 (2 x 1-inch/5 x 2.5-cm) pieces orange zest (see note)
2 to 3 dried red chili peppers, halved crosswise (optional)
2 green onions, chopped, white and green portions separated
2 tablespoons cornstarch

TO FINISH
2 teaspoons cornstarch whisked with 2 tablespoons water to make a slurry (optional)
Toasted sesame seeds, for garnish

1 Toss the chicken with 1 tablespoon orange juice, soy sauce and cooking wine in a medium bowl.
2 Make the sauce. Stir together the ¼ cup (60 ml) orange juice, soy sauce, cooking wine, sesame oil, rice vinegar and sugar in a small bowl.
3 Select SAUTÉ and set to HIGH/MORE. Add the vegetable oil. When the pot is hot, add the garlic, ginger, orange zest, chilies and white portions of the green onions, and stir and cook until fragrant, 30 seconds to 1 minute.
4 Just before cooking, toss the chicken with the cornstarch and add to the pot. Stir and cook until golden on most sides, 2 to 3 minutes. Press CANCEL.
5 Stir in the sauce and mix well, scraping the bottom of the pot to remove any cooked-on bits and avoid the BURN

warning.
6 Lock the lid. Select PRESSURE COOK/ MANUAL and set to HIGH for 3 minutes. Make sure the steam release valve is sealed. Once pressurized (8 to 10 minutes), the cook cycle will start.
7 When the timer beeps, let the pressure release naturally for 5 minutes. Then quick release any remaining pressure. When the float valve drops, press CANCEL and open the lid.
8 If you'd like a thicker sauce, select SAUTÉ and set to MEDIUM/NORMAL. Gradually pour the slurry into the pot, stirring until the sauce thickens to your liking. Keep in mind that the sauce will thicken even more when left to stand.
9 Garnish with the remaining green onions and sesame seeds, and serve with steamed rice and a side of vegetables.

> NOTES: Dried tangerine peel is often used in Chinese cooking. While you can dry peels yourself to intensify the flavor, fresh orange zest works as well. Use a peeler to remove 5 pieces of orange zest measuring about 2 x 1 inches (5 x 2.5 cm) each. You don't have to be exact. When zesting the orange, avoid the bitter white pith.

Chicken and Egg Rice Bowls — Oyako Donburi

A popular comfort food, this dish is usually made in individual portions. The chicken, mushrooms and egg are cooked separately in a sauce that's slipped on top of a bowl of rice. The Instant Pot® version looks a little messier but tastes just as good! Feel free to use beef instead of chicken or winter squash like kabocha for a veggie version.

PREP TIME: 15 minutes **TOTAL TIME:** 30 minutes
MAKES: 4 servings

1½ cups (300 g) uncooked Japanese-Style short-grain rice
Water
¼ cup (60 ml) soy sauce
2 tablespoons mirin
2 tablespoons sake or dry sherry
2 tablespoons granulated sugar
1½ cups (360 ml) Dashi (page 23) or low-sodium chicken stock
¾ pound (350 g) boneless, skinless chicken thighs or breasts, cut into ½-inch-thick (1.25-cm) slices
3 cups (340 g) sliced yellow onion (1 large)
8 small rehydrated (page 37) black mushrooms, stemmed and halved (2 ounces/60 g)
4 large eggs, lightly beaten

TO FINISH
1 cup green onions cut into 2-inch (5-cm) pieces, plus more for garnish
Shichimi togarashi ("Seven peppers" Japanese spice mixture, optional)

SPECIAL EQUIPMENT
7-inch (17.5-cm) heatproof container like a ceramic soufflé dish or cake tin
Steamer rack
Glass lid

1 Rinse the rice 2 to 3 times until it runs clear. Cover the rice with enough water to submerge by ½ inch (1.25 cm) and soak while you prepare the rest of the ingredients.

2 Stir together the soy sauce, mirin, sake, sugar and dashi in the pot. Taste and adjust with more soy sauce or sugar as desired. The sauce should have a balanced sweet-and-salty flavor. Add the chicken, onion and mushrooms and stir to mix.

3 Nestle a steamer rack inside above the chicken. Drain the rice in a fine-mesh strainer and tip into a heatproof container. Place the container on the rack and pour 1½ cups (360 ml) water over the rice.

4 Lock the lid. Select PRESSURE COOK/MANUAL and set to HIGH for 4 minutes. Make sure the steam release valve is sealed. Once pressurized (10 to 12 minutes), the cook cycle will start.

5 When the timer beeps, manually release the pressure. When the float valve drops, press CANCEL and open the lid.

6 Wearing heatproof mitts, remove the rice and steamer rack.

7 Select SAUTÉ and set to MEDIUM/NORMAL. Pour the eggs into the pot in a thin, steady stream, holding chopsticks or a fork over the edge of bowl to help distribute the eggs evenly. Add the green onions. Cover with a glass lid and cook until the eggs are set, 1 to 2 minutes for runny eggs (which I prefer) or 3 to 4 minutes for medium-firm.

8 Scoop the cooked rice into 4 large bowls. Divide the chicken and egg mixture (don't mix!) among the four bowls, followed by sauce. The sauce should soak through and flavor the rice. Garnish with more green onions and *shichimi togarashi* if desired.

Chicken Adobo

This is by far the most famous and most popular of all Filipino dishes. But every Filipino cook has his or her own version. The most popular ratio of soy sauce to vinegar in adobo is 1 to 2. It may seem like a lot of vinegar, but the long cooking time (at least 1 hour) mellows the tang of the vinegar and the chicken ends up falling-off-the-bone tender. The Instant Pot® definitely speeds up this process.

PREP TIME: 10 minutes TOTAL TIME: 60 minutes
MAKES: 4 to 6 servings

1½ cups (300 g) jasmine rice
6 medium garlic cloves, peeled and smashed
2 dried bay leaves
1 teaspoon black peppercorns or ½ teaspoon ground black pepper
1 teaspoon brown sugar, or more to taste (optional)
½ cup (120 ml) apple cider vinegar
¼ cup (60 ml) soy sauce
2 cups (480 ml) water, divided
8 bone-in, skin-on chicken legs or drumsticks and/or thighs (3 to 4 pounds/1.5 to 2 kg)
Chopped green onions, for garnish

SPECIAL EQUIPMENT
7- or 8-inch (17.5- to 20-cm) heatproof container (I use a 2-quart/2-l ceramic soufflé dish)
Steamer rack

> **NOTES:** Using the pot-in-pot method results in rice that's softer than usual because it cooks longer (see page 12 for more PIP tips).
>
> Feel free to combine chicken and pork together in one dish.

1 Rinse the rice 2 to 3 times until it runs clear. Drain in a fine-mesh strainer while you prepare the rest of the ingredients.

2 Stir together the garlic, bay leaves, peppercorns, sugar, vinegar, soy sauce and ½ cup (120 ml) water in the pot. Use tongs to coat the chicken on both sides with the sauce. Try to fit the chicken in one layer.

3 Nestle a steamer rack inside with the chicken. Tip the rice into a heatproof container and place it on the steamer rack. Pour 1½ cups (360 ml) water over the rice.

4 Lock the lid. Select PRESSURE COOK/MANUAL and set to HIGH for 15 minutes. Make sure the steam release valve is sealed. Once pressurized (12 to 15 minutes), the cook cycle will start.

5 When the timer beeps, let the pressure release naturally for 10 minutes. Then quick release any remaining pressure. When the float valve drops, press CANCEL and open the lid.

6 Wearing heatproof mitts, remove the rice and steamer rack.

7 Insert an instant-read thermometer into the chicken at its thickest part. The temperature should read at least 165° F (71° Celsius). If not, select PRESSURE COOK/MANUAL again for another minute or two. It will take much less time to build up pressure the second time since the food is already hot.

8 When the timer beeps again, manually release the pressure. When the float valve drops, press CANCEL and open the lid.

9 Now, you have two options: Using tongs, transfer the chicken to a broiler pan lined with foil. Broil the chicken in the middle rack for 3 to 5 minutes. Or, you can transfer the chicken to a serving dish and serve as is. Tent with foil to keep warm.

10 Select SAUTÉ and set to HIGH/MORE. Reduce the sauce for 10 to 15 minutes until you're happy.

11 Strain the sauce through a fine-mesh sieve to catch any solids. Skim off fat from the surface.

12 Drizzle the sauce over the chicken and sprinkle with green onions. Serve with the rice and a side of vegetables.

Chicken Rendang Curry   Rendang Ayam

Similar to a Thai red curry, *rendang* is a slow-cooked dish that requires hours of stovetop nursing. It was only when I bought an Instant Pot® that I even entertained the idea of making it myself. And when I did, I decided to make a chicken version rather than the usual beef rendang. I prefer using chicken thighs because they don't dry out as easily, but use chicken breasts if you prefer them.

PREP TIME: 20 minutes **TOTAL TIME:** 1 hour, 5 minutes **MAKES:** 4 to 6 servings

SPICE PASTE

2 cups roughly chopped shallots or red onion (6 ounces/180 g)

5 medium garlic cloves, peeled

1-inch (2.5-cm) knob fresh ginger, peeled and roughly chopped

1-inch (2.5-cm) piece fresh galangal (page 19), peeled and chopped

1 plump lemongrass stalk, prepped (page 58) and chopped into rings

3 fresh long red chilies trimmed, seeded if desired, and chopped

3 tablespoons ground red chili powder (see notes)

1 teaspoon ground turmeric

2 teaspoons fine sea salt

1½ to 2 pounds (675 to 900 g) boneless, skinless chicken thighs or breasts

1 (13½-ounce/400-ml) can coconut milk (unshaken)

1-inch (2.5-cm) piece galangal, peeled and sliced into 3 or 4 coins

1 plump lemongrass stalk, prepped (page 58) chopped into 3 sections

5 Asian lime leaves, torn in half and crumpled to release essential oils, or zest from 1 large lime

1 tablespoon coconut sugar or 2 teaspoons brown sugar

⅓ cup (35 g) finely shredded unsweetened coconut (optional)

1   Make the spice paste. Blitz the shallots, garlic, ginger, galangal, turmeric, fresh chilies, chili powder and salt in a food processor until a coarse paste forms. Add water, 1 tablespoon at a time, to loosen the paste as needed.

2   Select SAUTÉ and set to MEDIUM/NORMAL. Add 2 tablespoons of oil. When the pot is hot, add the spice paste, stir and cook until it turns a few shades darker, and the oil separates from the paste forming two distinct layers, 3 to 4 minutes. If the paste starts to burn at any time, adjust to LOW/LESS. Press CANCEL.

3   Scoop the thick cream from the top of the coconut milk into a bowl. Pour ¾ cup of the thin coconut milk into the pot. Add the galangal, lemongrass, lime leaves and coconut sugar. Mix well, scraping the bottom of the pot to remove any cooked-on bits and avoid the BURN warning.

4   Coat both sides of the chicken with sauce. Nestle the chicken into the sauce, preferably in one layer.

5   Lock the lid. Select PRESSURE COOK/MANUAL and set to HIGH for 10 minutes. Make sure the steam release valve is sealed. Once pressurized (10 to 12 minutes), the cook cycle will start.

6   While the chicken is cooking, toast the shredded coconut in a dry skillet on the stovetop over medium-low heat until it turns light brown and aromatic, about 3 minutes. (This can be done ahead and refrigerated or frozen.)

7   When the timer beeps, let the pressure release naturally (20 to 30 minutes). When the float valve drops, press CANCEL and open the lid.

8   Carefully remove the chicken to a plate. Cut it up into smaller pieces if you like, but don't shred it. Tent with foil to keep warm.

9   Select SAUTÉ and set to MEDIUM/NORMAL. Add the remaining coconut cream and milk and ¾ of the toasted coconut and cook for 2 to 3 minutes, stirring constantly. If you'd like a drier curry, simmer the sauce until reduced by about one-third, 10 to 15 minutes. Note that the sauce will thicken as it cools. Remove the herbs.

10 Add the chicken back to the sauce and adjust to LOW/LESS to heat the chicken through.

11 Garnish with the remaining shredded coconut and serve with steamed rice and a vegetable side dish. Or let it sit in the refrigerator overnight—*rendang* always tastes better the next day!

NOTES: I use a mix of 1½ teaspoons cayenne [spicy], 1 tablespoon ancho [medium spicy] and 1 tablespoon plus 1½ teaspoons paprika [not spicy].

You can also use bone-in chicken parts for this dish. Increase cooking time to 15 minutes.

No fresh chilies? Add 1 more tablespoon chili powder.

To make beef *rendang*, use 2 pounds beef chuck cut into 3-inch (7.5-cm) pieces and cook at HIGH PRESSURE for 20 minutes.

Yellow Chicken Curry Ca Ri Ga

Use any type of curry powder or paste that you have for this simple Vietnamese-Style curry.

PREP TIME: 25 minutes **TOTAL TIME:** 60 minutes
MAKES: 4 servings

1 tablespoon vegetable oil
¼ cup chopped shallots
1 tablespoon minced garlic (3 medium cloves)
2 tablespoons curry powder, preferably Vietnamese or Madras
1 teaspoon fine sea salt
2½ to 3 pounds (1.4 kg) bone-in chicken drumsticks and thighs
1½ cups (360 g) chopped onion
2 plump lemongrass stalks, prepped (page 58), smashed with a pestle or meat tenderizer, and cut into thirds
1½ cups (360 ml) low-sodium chicken stock
1½ pounds (720 g) sweet potatoes, peeled and cut into 1½-inch (6.25-cm) chunks
1 (13½-ounce/400-ml) can coconut milk, shaken
2 tablespoons fish sauce

1 Select SAUTÉ and set to HIGH/MORE. Add the oil. When the pot is hot, add the shallots and garlic, and stir until fragrant, about 30 seconds. Add the curry powder and salt and stir until fragrant, 1 minute.
2 Add the chicken and stir to coat. Sear for 3 to 4 minutes on each side to prevent the meat from falling apart during cooking. Don't worry about completely cooking the chicken at this point. Add the onion and stir to mix. Press CANCEL.
3 Add the lemongrass and stock, and stir, scraping the bottom of the pot to remove any cooked-on bits and avoid the BURN warning.
4 Lock the lid. Select PRESSURE COOK/MANUAL and set to HIGH for 8 minutes. Make sure the steam release valve is sealed. Once pressurized (16 to 18 minutes), the cook cycle will start.
5 When the timer beeps, let the pressure

release naturally for 10 minutes. Then quick release any remaining pressure. When the float valve drops, press CANCEL and open the lid.
6 Tip in the sweet potatoes. Select PRESSURE COOK/MANUAL and set to HIGH PRESSURE for 0 MINUTES. Make sure the steam release valve is sealed. It will take less time to pressurize the second time since the food is already hot.
7 When the timer beeps again, manually release the pressure. When the float valve drops, press CANCEL and open the lid.
8 Select SAUTÉ and set to MEDIUM/NORMAL. Stir in the coconut milk and simmer for 3 to 4 minutes, or until the curry reaches your desired consistency. Season with the fish sauce.
9 Serve immediately with a freshly baked baguette or over rice. Or let the flavors meld overnight.

> **NOTES:** If you like it spicy, add a few dried chilies or some cayenne.
>   For a lighter option, reduce the coconut milk in half and substitute with more chicken stock.
>   You can also use cut carrots or potatoes instead of sweet potatoes. If using potatoes, set the cook time to 1 minute at HIGH PRESSURE.
>   Or try whole fingerling or new potatoes and cook them together with the chicken.
>   Like all curries, this dish will taste better the following day.

Chicken and Mushroom "Stroganoff"

This childhood favorite of mine is almost like a stroganoff but minus the cream. The Asian flavors are livened up with a little brandy although cognac, sherry or Chinese cooking wine work well too. My mom occasionally added a surprise to the dish: chicken livers. I didn't appreciate liver as a child but love it now. It's really delicious when prepared correctly.

PREP TIME: 10 minutes **TOTAL TIME:** 30 minutes
MAKES: 4 servings

1 tablespoon vegetable oil

1 tablespoon minced garlic (3 medium cloves)

1-inch (2.5-cm) knob fresh ginger, peeled and cut into matchsticks

1½ cups (240 g) sliced onion

1 pound (450 g) boneless, skinless chicken thighs, cut into 1-inch (2.5-cm) cubes

4 ounces (120 g) cremini mushrooms, sliced (1 cup)

1 tablespoon brandy

¼ cup (60 ml) oyster sauce

1 tablespoon sweet soy sauce (or 1 tablespoon soy sauce plus 1 tablespoon brown sugar)

4 ounces (120 g) chicken liver, soaked in cold water for about 15 minutes (optional)

> **NOTES:** Only a few seconds separate soft, tender liver from tough, crumbly liver. So please pay attention and don't over cook it!

1 Select SAUTÉ and set to HIGH/MORE. Add the vegetable oil. When the pot is hot, add the garlic, ginger and onion, and stir and cook until the onion has softened, about 2 to 3 minutes.

2 Add the chicken, mushrooms and brandy, and stir and cook for about 1 minute to burn off some of the alcohol. Press CANCEL.

3 Stir in the oyster sauce and sweet soy sauce and mix well, scraping the bottom of the pot to remove any cooked-on bits and avoid the BURN warning.

4 Lock the lid. Select PRESSURE COOK/MANUAL and set to HIGH for 3 minutes. Make sure the steam release valve is sealed. Once pressurized (8 to 10 minutes), the cook cycle will start.

5 While the chicken is cooking, prepare the liver if using. Wash the livers and pat dry with a paper towel. Remove and discard the connective tissue, then cut into bite-sized slices.

6 When the timer beeps, let the pressure release naturally for 5 minutes. Then quick release any remaining pressure. When the float valve drops, press CANCEL and open the lid.

7 If using liver, select SAUTÉ and set to MEDIUM/NORMAL. Add the liver and gently stir and cook until barely done (I like it still pink inside), 2 to 3 minutes. Don't overcook or it will be crumbly and mealy. Press CANCEL.

8 Serve immediately with steamed rice and a vegetable side.

Pork Dishes

Pork is prominent in Asian cooking. The shoulder, butt and belly are particularly popular cuts. Cooking them in the Instant Pot® makes them melt-in-the-mouth tender in no time at all.

Marinated Pork Bulgogi

Bulgogi is a Korean dish of meat marinated in a sweet-and-savory sauce and grilled or cooked on a stovetop griddle. In the pressure cooker, the meat cooks up tasty and tender, but you'll need to take an extra step to get the caramelized coating on the meat. I prefer pork to beef; it's usually spicier, thanks to the addition of gochujang and gochugaru, and not as sweet. Adjust the level of spiciness to your taste; you can even omit the red pepper entirely.

PREP TIME: 5 minutes **TOTAL TIME:** 40 minutes, plus marinating time **MAKES:** 4 to 6 servings

1 pound (450 g) pork shoulder or tenderloin, cut into 2 x 1 x ⅛ inch (5 cm x 2.5 cm x 3 mm) slices
1½ cups (240 g) sliced onion

MARINADE
1 tablespoon minced garlic
1 tablespoon minced fresh ginger
1 tablespoon soy sauce
1 tablespoon mirin
1 tablespoon sesame oil
1½ teaspoons light brown sugar
½ teaspoon fine sea salt
2 tablespoons gochujang
1 to 3 teaspoons gochugaru

GARNISH
1 tablespoon sesame seeds
2 tablespoons chopped green onions

1 Toss the pork and onions with the marinade: garlic, ginger, soy sauce, mirin, sesame oil, sugar, salt, gojuchang and gochugaru. Marinate in the refrigerator for at least one hour if possible, up to 24 hours.
2 Tip the marinated pork, onion and juices into the pot. Lock the lid. Select PRESSURE COOK/MANUAL and set to HIGH for 12 minutes. Make sure the steam release valve is sealed. Once pressurized (6 to 7 minutes), the cook cycle will start.
3 When the timer beeps, let the pressure release naturally for 10 minutes. Then quick release any remaining pressure. When the float valve drops, press CANCEL and open the lid.
4 Scoop the pork and onions onto a serving plate using a slotted spoon. Tent with foil to keep warm. Skim the fat from the sauce.
5 Select SAUTÉ and set to HIGH/MORE. Reduce the sauce, stirring occasionally, for 5 to 7 minutes, or until your desired consistency.
6 Optional step: When ready to serve, place the top rack in your oven 4 inches (10 cm) from the heat source and turn on the broiler. Toss the pork and onion slices with about ¼ cup (60 ml) sauce so they're lightly coated but not dripping. Spread in one layer on a foil-lined rimmed baking sheet, and broil until caramelized and lightly charred, 3 to 4 minutes, flipping halfway.
7 Sprinkle with sesame seeds and green onions, and serve with steamed rice and the rest of the sauce from the pressure cooker on the side. Other options: Wrap the meat in lettuce leaves or make Korean Bibimbap Mixed Rice Bowl (page 64).

> **NOTES:** Instead of pork, you can use beef sirloin or chicken thighs. If you're using chicken, leave the thighs whole and cook for 10 minutes under high pressure. Slice right before serving.

Spare Ribs with Black Bean Sauce

My husband jokes that when we go out for dim sum with my family, he has to prepare himself for the "battle of the chopsticks." If you aren't quick with your chopsticks, you'll be left with nothing to eat. One of my favorite dim sum dishes is tiny pork ribs steamed with black bean sauce. Ask your butcher to cut up the ribs for you.

PREP TIME: 5 minutes TOTAL TIME: 45 minutes
MAKES: 4 to 6 servings

2 tablespoons prepared black bean garlic sauce
1 tablespoon Chinese cooking wine
1 teaspoon soy sauce
1 tablespoon minced garlic (3 medium cloves)
1 tablespoon grated fresh ginger
2 teaspoons sesame oil
2 teaspoons granulated sugar
1 tablespoon cornstarch
1½ pounds (720 g) pork ribs, cut into 1-inch (2.5-cm) pieces
Chopped green onions, for garnish

SPECIAL EQUIPMENT
7- to 8-inch (17.5- to 20-cm) heatproof container or bowl (I use a 7-inch/17.5-cm metal cake tin)
Steamer rack

NOTES: The type of bowl you use will make a difference in the overall cooking time. If you're using an oven-safe glass or ceramic bowl instead of a metal one, add 5 minutes to the cooking time.

1 Mix together the black bean sauce, cooking wine, soy sauce, garlic, ginger, sesame oil and sugar in a large bowl. Add the pork and toss to coat. Refrigerate for at least 30 minutes.
2 Toss the marinated pork with the cornstarch and transfer to a heatproof container. Cover with foil.
3 Pour 1 cup water into the pot and nestle a steamer rack inside. Place the ribs on the rack.
4 Lock the lid. Select PRESSURE COOK/

MANUAL and set to HIGH for 25 minutes. Make sure the steam release valve is sealed. Once pressurized (10 to 12 minutes), the cook cycle will start.
5 When the timer beeps, let the pressure release naturally (10 to 15 minutes). When the float valve drops, press CANCEL and open the lid.
6 Carefully remove the ribs using heatproof mittens. Garnish with green onions and serve immediately with steamed rice and a vegetable side dish.

Honey Garlic Pork Chops

Over the years, I've tried making honey garlic pork chops at home with varying success. This satisfying Instant Pot® version is now a go-to weeknight meal when I'm in a hurry to put dinner on the table.

PREP TIME: 10 minutes TOTAL TIME: 35 minutes

Four (1-inch-thick/2.5-cm) boneless pork loin chops (preferably
  with some marbling, about 1½
  pounds/720 g)
Fine sea salt and freshly ground black
  pepper
½ cup (65 g) cornstarch, for dredging
Vegetable oil
2 tablespoons minced garlic (6 medium
  cloves)
2 teaspoons cornstarch mixed with 2
  tablespoons water to make a slurry
  (optional)

SAUCE
¼ cup (60 ml) low-sodium chicken
  stock
¼ cup (60 ml) honey
1 tablespoon soy sauce
2 teaspoons rice vinegar
1 tablespoon light brown sugar

SPECIAL EQUIPMENT
Drop lid (page 11)

1 Make the sauce. Whisk together the stock, honey, soy sauce, rice vinegar and sugar in a medium bowl.

2 Pat the pork chops very dry with paper towels and season both sides generously with salt and pepper. Dredge in the cornstarch, making sure to cover the edges, and shake any excess off. Discard the remaining cornstarch.

3 Select SAUTÉ and set to HIGH/MORE. Add 2 tablespoons vegetable oil. When the pot is hot, add two pork chops and sear until lightly browned but still pink on the inside, 2 to 3 minutes on each side. Remove to a plate. Add 1 more tablespoon (or more) oil and repeat with the remaining pork. Remove.

4 Add the garlic and stir and cook until fragrant, about 30 seconds. Pour in the sauce and mix well, scraping the bottom of the pot to remove any cooked-on bits and avoid the BURN warning.

5 Arrange the pork in one layer in the pot and pour in any juices. Place a drop lid on top.

6 Lock the lid. Select PRESSURE COOK/

MANUAL and set to LOW for 0 minutes. Make sure the steam release valve is sealed. Once pressurized (6 to 7 minutes), the cook cycle will start.

7 When the timer beeps, let the pressure release naturally for 10 minutes. Then quick release any remaining pressure. When the float valve drops, press CANCEL and open the lid.

8 Insert an instant-read thermometer into a pork chop; it should read at least 145° F (63° C). I like my chops with a slight blush in the center, but cook them for 1 or 2 minutes more if you prefer.

9 Remove the pork to a serving plate and tent with foil to keep warm.

10 Select SAUTÉ and set to HIGH/MORE. Reduce the sauce until it's the consistency of thin gravy, 3 to 4 minutes. If necessary, stir in the cornstarch slurry to thicken it to your liking. Keep in mind the sauce will continue to thicken as it stands. Taste and adjust the seasonings if desired. Press CANCEL.

11 Pour the sauce over the pork and serve with steamed rice and vegetables.

> **NOTES:** When I can't find 1-inch-thick (2.5-cm) boneless pork chops, I will buy a hunk of shoulder or loin and slice it to the desired thickness. Or just ask your butcher to help you!

Chinese "Red Cooked" Pork Hong Shao Rou

Every Chinese family has their own rendition of red cooked pork using a cornucopia of spices ranging from star anise to cinnamon to orange peel. The Vietnamese make a similar dish using coconut water and fish sauce. My mom's version uses Indonesian sweet soy sauce. For variety, you can add hard-boiled eggs and tofu to the sauce. Or you can substitute chicken or duck. The variations are endless, and there's no right or wrong way to make this dish. So feel free to create your own version!

PREP TIME: 5 minutes **TOTAL TIME:** 50 minutes
MAKES: 4 to 6 servings

2 tablespoons brown sugar
1½ to 2 pounds (900 g) pork belly, cut into 1½-inch (3.75-cm) square pieces
¼ cup (60 ml) Chinese cooking wine
2 tablespoons soy sauce
1 tablespoon dark soy sauce
2 star anise pods
2-inch (5-cm) piece cinnamon stick
1 cup (240 ml) water
½ cup green onions cut into 2-inch (5-cm) pieces (optional)

NOTES: My recipe tester Lenny offers these suggestions:
· Add a few slices of ginger and some orange peel to flavor the sauce.
· Reduce the sauce on the stovetop— it's faster and more efficient!

1 Select SAUTÉ and set to LOW/LESS. When the pot is hot, stir together the sugar and 2 tablespoons water. Cook until the sugar melts into a syrup, stirring occasionally. When the syrup turns golden, add the pork and stir to coat. Keep stirring until the pork is browned on all sides with barely any pink remaining, 3 to 5 minutes. Press CANCEL.

2 Add the cooking wine, soy sauce, dark soy sauce, star anise, cinnamon and water. Mix well.

3 Lock the lid. Select PRESSURE COOK/MANUAL and set to HIGH for 20 minutes.

Make sure the steam release valve is sealed. Once pressurized (7 to 10 minutes), the cook cycle will start.

4 When the timer beeps, let the pressure release naturally (10 to 15 minutes). When the float valve drops, press CANCEL and open the lid. Skim off the fat from the surface.

5 Select SAUTÉ and set to HIGH/MORE. Keep stirring to reduce the sauce to your liking and/or until it coats the pork.

6 Garnish with the green onions if using and serve with steamed rice or steamed buns.

Japanese-Style Braised Pork Belly

The dishes *chashu* and *kakuni* basically use the same ingredients and have a similar cooking method. The big difference is their shape. For *chashu*, a pork belly slab is rolled lengthwise into a cylinder and tied firmly with kitchen twine before braising in liquid. When cooked, the belly is cut into rounds. *Kakuni* literally means "square simmered" and yes, (almost) square bite-sized pieces of pork are simmered in a braising liquid. To make things simple, I used the strips of pork belly sold at my local Asian market (they're about 2½ x 1 x 10 inches, or 6.25 x 2.5 x 25 cm). I prefer belly without skin, but feel free to leave the skin on if you prefer.

PREP TIME: 10 minutes **TOTAL TIME:** 116 minutes
MAKES: 6 servings of pork belly; 7 to 8 cups ramen broth

2 pounds (900 g) boneless pork belly, skin removed, cut into approximately 4 (2½-inch-wide/6.25-cm) strips
2 tablespoons vegetable oil
1 large onion, roughly chopped (12 ounces/360 g)
6 medium garlic cloves, peeled and smashed
3-inch (7.5-cm) knob ginger, peeled and roughly sliced
8 cups (2 l) water
6 green onions, white parts only (1½ cups/45 g, reserve greens and light green parts for garnishing ramen bowls)
4 x 4-inch (10 x 10-cm) piece of *kombu/kelp*

SAUCE
½ cup (120 ml) soy sauce
½ cup (120 ml) mirin
¼ cup (60 ml) sake
¼ cup (50 g) granulated sugar
1½ cups (360 ml) low-sodium chicken stock

SPECIAL EQUIPMENT
Drop lid (page 11)

1 Remove the pork belly from the refrigerator an hour before cooking.

2 Select SAUTÉ and set to HIGH/MORE. Add the vegetable oil. When the pot is hot, add the onions, garlic and ginger and cook and stir until charred on most sides, about 10 minutes. Adjust the heat to MEDIUM/NORMAL if it starts smoking excessively. Pour in 1 cup (240 ml) water and scrape the bottom of the pot to remove any cooked-on bits and avoid the BURN warning. Press CANCEL.

3 Add the white portions of green onions, and *kombu* (if using), to the pressure cooker. Pour in 8 cups (2 l) water.

4 Lock the lid. Select PRESSURE COOK/MANUAL and set to HIGH for 60 minutes. Make sure the steam release valve is sealed. Once pressurized (20 to 25 minutes), the cook cycle will start.

5 When the timer beeps, let the pressure release naturally (30 to 35 minutes). When the float valve drops, press CANCEL and open the lid.

6 Remove the pork belly to a plate. Strain the liquid through a fine-mesh strainer into a large bowl. Discard the solids. You'll have about 7 to 8 cups (1.7 to 2 l) pork broth to make ramen.

7 Skim off the fat from the surface with a ladle and discard. If you're not using the broth right away, refrigerate for several hours or overnight. The fat will solidify, making it easier to remove. The broth will keep in the refrigerator for up to 5 days or in the freezer for 1 month.

8 Make the sauce. Mix together the soy sauce, mirin, sake, sugar and 1½ cups chicken stock. Return the cooked pork belly to the Instant Pot® and place a drop lid on top.

9 Lock the lid. Select PRESSURE COOK/MANUAL and set to HIGH for 10 minutes. Make sure the steam release valve is sealed. Once pressurized (6 to 8 minutes), the cook cycle will start.

10 When the timer beeps, manually release the pressure. When the float valve drops, press CANCEL and open the lid.

11 Rest the belly in the pot for 20 minutes. Remove and let it cool to room temperature. Strain the braising liquid through a paper-towel-lined strainer into a bowl. Refrigerate for several hours, then remove the fat that solidifies on top. Reserve for making Shoyu Tare Sauce (page 60), Japanese-Style Soy Sauce Eggs (page 28) and Seasoned Bamboo Shoots (page 29), and for drizzling.

12 When the belly has cooled, refrigerate in a sealed container until it's chilled through. The pork belly must be chilled thoroughly before slicing, or you'll end up with pulled pork.

13 When ready to serve, place the pork belly on a cutting board. Slice into 2 x 1½ x ½-inch-thick (5 x 3.75 x 1.25-cm) pieces.

14 You have several options for reheating the pork belly slices:
· Reheat in the ramen soup broth with noodles and other garnishes.
· Reheat with a small amount of braising liquid in a skillet until hot.
· Reheat under a broiler (or with a blowtorch if you have one!) to char its surface.

15 Use the pork belly slices to top ramen bowls (page 60), stuff into sandwiches or eat with rice drizzled with sauce and vegetables.

NOTES: The pork will keep for a week in the fridge, or you can freeze it for 2 months. You can also use pork shoulder or pork loin in this recipe.

It's best to cook pork belly a day or two before you're planning to serve it so that the flavors meld and the solidified fat can be removed from the surface of the braising liquid. This is important especially if you're making ramen bowls (pages 60).

Sweet and Sour Pork

Making sweet and sour pork at home is easy. The original deep-fried version, though tasty, is messy and time-consuming. This Instant Pot® version is healthier and quicker to cook. The end result will not be as crispy as the deep-fried version, but it's still delicious! Use chicken if you prefer.

PREP TIME: 15 minutes **TOTAL TIME:** 37 minutes
MAKES: 4 to 6 servings

1 pound (450 g) pork shoulder or boneless loin chops, cut into 1-inch (2.5-cm) cubes
2 tablespoons all-purpose flour
2 tablespoons cornstarch
½ teaspoon fine sea salt
¼ teaspoon freshly ground pepper
2 tablespoons plus 1 teaspoon vegetable oil, divided

SAUCE
¼ cup (60 ml) tomato ketchup
¼ cup (60 ml) canned pineapple juice
2 tablespoons white vinegar
1 teaspoon Chinese cooking wine
1 tablespoon soy sauce
2 teaspoons granulated sugar
2 teaspoons minced garlic
1 large carrot, peeled and sliced into 1-inch (2.5-cm) pieces
1 red or green bell pepper, cut into 2-inch (5-cm) squares
1 medium yellow onion, cut into 8 wedges and separated
1 cup (165 g) canned pineapple chunks in juice, well-drained (reserve ¼ cup [60 ml] juice for the sauce above)

TO FINISH
2 teaspoons cornstarch mixed with 2 tablespoons water to form a slurry (optional)
Chopped green onions, to garnish

SPECIAL EQUIPMENT
Paper towels
Large plate

1 Toss the pork together with the flour, cornstarch, salt and pepper in a medium bowl or ziptop bag. Bring the pork to room temperature before cooking.

2 Make the sauce. Stir together the ketchup, pineapple juice, vinegar, cooking wine, soy sauce and sugar in a medium bowl until the sugar dissolves. Taste and adjust the seasonings if desired.

3 Select SAUTÉ and set to HIGH/MORE. Add 2 tablespoons oil. When your pot is hot, sear the pork on all sides until barely pink, 2 to 3 minutes. Remove to a plate lined with paper towels.

4 Add 1 teaspoon oil followed by the garlic and stir and cook until fragrant, about 30 seconds. Add the carrot, bell pepper and onion, stirring between each addition. Press CANCEL.

5 Stir in the sauce and scrape the bottom of the pot to remove any cooked-on bits and avoid the BURN warning.

6 Return the pork to the pot, arranging the pieces in one layer on top of the vegetables and sauce. Don't mix.

7 Lock the lid. Select PRESSURE COOK/MANUAL and set to LOW for 0 minutes. Make sure the steam release valve is sealed. Once pressurized (7 to 10 minutes), the cook cycle will start.

8 When the timer beeps, let the pressure release naturally for 10 minutes. Then quick release any remaining pressure. When the float valve drops, press CANCEL and open the lid.

9 Using a slotted spoon, scoop the pork and vegetables into a serving bowl. Tent with foil to keep warm.

10 Select SAUTÉ and set to HIGH/MORE. Add the pineapple and cook and stir for 1 to 2 minutes to reduce the sauce. If you prefer a thicker sauce, gradually stir in the slurry. Spoon sauce and pineapple over the pork and vegetables. Garnish with green onions and serve with steamed rice.

HOW TO PREPARE THE PORK

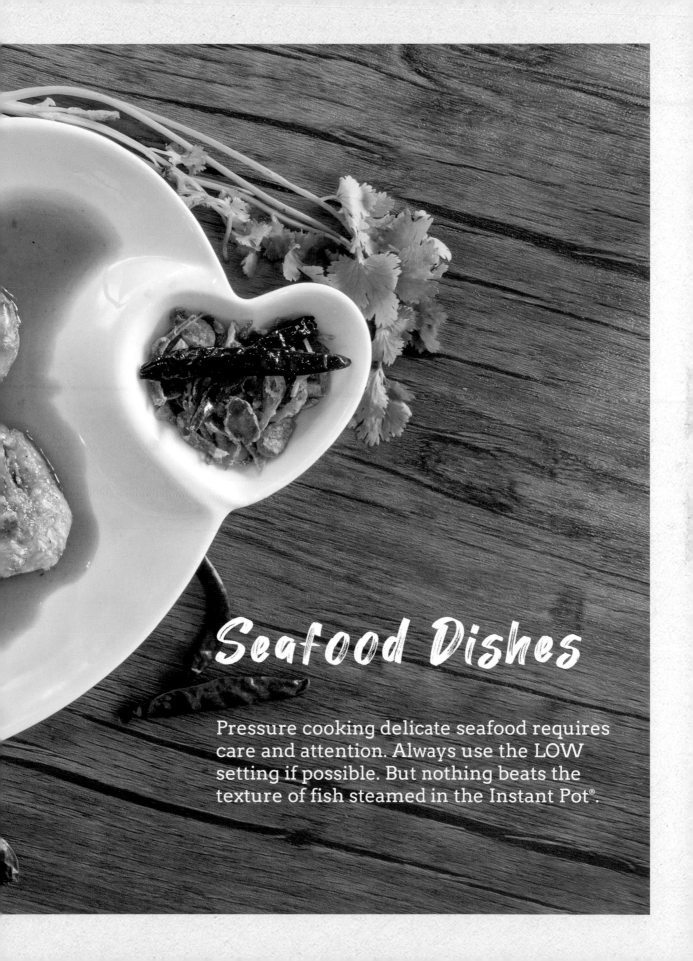

Seafood Dishes

Pressure cooking delicate seafood requires care and attention. Always use the LOW setting if possible. But nothing beats the texture of fish steamed in the Instant Pot®.

Green Curry Mussels

Most mussels are now farm-raised, so they're easier to clean. You should still take time to rinse them under cold running water, and be sure to remove the beards—those shaggy, seaweed-like strands—that are still attached to the shells.

PREP TIME: 10 minutes TOTAL TIME: 25 minutes
MAKES: 4 servings

2 tablespoons vegetable oil
1 tablespoon minced garlic
1 tablespoon grated fresh ginger
1 cup (240 g) chopped onion
1 to 2 tablespoons Thai green curry paste (depending on how spicy you like it)
1 cup (240 ml) coconut milk
½ cup (120 ml) low-sodium chicken stock
2 tablespoons fish sauce
1 tablespoon coconut sugar or 2 teaspoons light brown sugar
2 tablespoons freshly squeezed lime juice
2 pounds (900 g) mussels, scrubbed and debearded
1 cup loosely packed Thai basil leaves, divided
Lime wedges

1 Select SAUTÉ and set to MEDIUM/HIGH. Add the vegetable oil. When the pot is hot, add the garlic, ginger and onion and stir and cook until the onion is soft, 1 to 2 minutes.

2 Stir in the green curry paste and cook. Some of the paste will likely brown and stick to the pot, so scrape the bottom occasionally to make sure it doesn't burn. Add a little stock to loosen if necessary and/or adjust the heat to LOW/LESS. Cook until the paste turns a few shades darker and your kitchen fills with a pungent aroma, 2 to 3 minutes. Press CANCEL.

3 Pour in the coconut milk, stock, fish sauce and sugar. Tip in the mussels and mix.

4 Lock the lid. Select PRESSURE COOK/MANUAL and set to HIGH for 1 minute. Make sure the steam release valve is sealed. Once pressurized (10 to 15 minutes), the cook cycle will start.

5 When the timer beeps, manually release the pressure. When the float valve drops, press CANCEL and open the lid.

6 Discard any unopened shells. Add the lime juice and ¾ cup basil. Divide the mussels and coconut sauce among 4 bowls. Sprinkle with the remaining basil (thinly sliced), and serve with lime wedges and bread.

> **NOTES:** If you're short on time, simply cook the garlic, ginger, onion and curry paste together until fragrant, 1 to 2 minutes. Add the rest of the ingredients and lock on the lid.
>   If you'd like a little more heat, add 1 to 2 jalapeno peppers.

Tangy Tamarind Shrimp

Shrimp cook very quickly so remove them as soon as the timer beeps and only use bigger ones. If in doubt, err on the side of undercooking. You can continue to cook them in the residual heat after you press CANCEL, if necessary.

PREP TIME: 5 minutes **COOK TIME:** 10 minutes plus pressurizing time **MAKES:** 4 servings

1 pound (450 g) uncooked peeled and deveined shrimp (21/25 or larger size)

SAUCE
¼ cup (60 ml) tamarind extract (page 18)
4 teaspoons fish sauce
1 tablespoon honey
1 tablespoon brown sugar
1 tablespoon chili paste, like sriracha or *sambal oelek*
1 tablespoon vegetable oil
1 tablespoon minced garlic (3 medium cloves)
¼ cup chopped shallot (1 small/120 g)
Parsley and dried chilies for garnish, optional

1 Place the shrimp in a large bowl and sprinkle with salt. Pour in enough tap water to cover by ½ inch (1.25 cm). Swirl and set aside while you prepare the rest of the ingredients.

2 Make the sauce by whisking together the tamarind, fish sauce, honey, sugar and chili paste. Taste and adjust the sour, sweet, salty and spicy notes if desired.

3 Drain the shrimp and pat dry with paper towels.

4 Select SAUTÉ and set to NORMAL/MEDIUM. Add the vegetable oil. When the pot is hot, add the garlic and shallot and stir and cook until fragrant, about 30 seconds. Press CANCEL.

5 Add the sauce and shrimp. Stir to coat.

6 Lock the lid. Select PRESSURE COOK/MANUAL and set to LOW for 0 minutes. Make sure the steam release valve is sealed. Once pressurized (5 to 6 minutes), the cook cycle will start. When the timer beeps, manually release the pressure. When the float valve drops, press CANCEL and open the lid.

7 If you'd like a thicker sauce, scoop the shrimp into a serving bowl and tent with foil to keep warm. Select SAUTÉ and set to HIGH/MORE. Stir continuously until reduced to your liking. Pour the sauce over the shrimp. Sprinkle with parsley and dried chilies, if using, and serve with steamed white rice and a vegetable side dish.

> **NOTES:** Rinsing in salted water "perks up" the shrimp and gives it back its brininess.

Hot and Sour Salmon Soup   Sinigang

Filipino cuisine values sourness. Whether from vinegar, citrus or unripe fruits, sourness adds sparkle, helping balance intensely fishy flavors and rich, fatty meats. You can use pork or other seafood in this dish, but I love using salmon heads. Not only are salmon heads cheap, the cheeks are tender and tasty.

PREP TIME: 5 minutes TOTAL TIME: 30 minutes
MAKES: 4 to 6 servings

1 salmon head (about 1½ pounds/
   720 g)
1 tablespoon vegetable oil
1 small yellow or red onion, sliced into
   eighths (4 ounces/120 g)
1 tablespoon minced garlic (3 medium
   cloves)
5 cups (1.2 l) low sodium fish or chicken
   stock
¼ cup (60 ml) plus 1 tablespoon tamarind extract (page 18)
¼ cup (60 ml) fish sauce
1 to 2 Thai chilies, slit lengthwise
   (optional)
8 ounces (200 g) daikon radish or
   turnips, peeled, and cut into 1-inch
   (2.5-cm) pieces
2 medium Roma tomatoes (4 ounces
   /60 g), cored and cut into quarters
1 medium eggplant, cut into 1-inch (2.5-
   cm) slices (about 8 ounces/200 g)
2 ounces (60 g) green beans, trimmed
   and halved if large

TO FINISH
Freshly squeezed lime juice, as needed
Freshly ground black pepper

1 Cut the salmon head in half, or have the fishmonger do this. Wash well to remove any blood or gills. Gills will ruin the broth by making it bitter and cloudy.

2 Select SAUTÉ and set to HIGH/MORE. Add the oil. When the pot is hot, add the garlic and onion, and stir and cook until the onion has softened, 3 to 5 minutes.

3 Add the salmon head, and sear on each side for 1 to 2 minutes. Press CANCEL.

4 Add the stock, tamarind, fish sauce and Thai chili, if using. Scrape the bottom of the pot to remove any cooked-on bits and avoid the BURN warning. Add the daikon, tomatoes and eggplant.

5 Lock the lid. Select PRESSURE COOK/ MANUAL and set to LOW for 3 minutes. Make sure the steam release valve is sealed. Once pressurized (20 to 25 min-utes), the cook cycle will start.

6 When the timer beeps, manually release the pressure. When the float valve drops, press CANCEL and open the lid.

7 Check for doneness with a fork. If the fish flakes easily, it's done. I like my salmon medium-rare. If it's not cooked to your liking, cover the pot and cook in the residual heat for another minute or two.

8 Remove the salmon head and pick out all the meat, especially the cheek meat. Place in a large serving bowl, or divide into individual bowls.

9 Stir the green beans into the soup and cook in the residual heat. Taste and season with additional fish sauce or lime juice as needed. Ladle into the bowls or individual bowls, sprinkle with pepper and serve with steamed rice.

NOTES: If you prefer salmon fillets to the head, use ¾-pound (360 g) belly-cut salmon cut into 2-inch (5-cm) pieces instead.

My recipe tester Betty Ann shares that in the Philippines *sinigang* is usually cooked with backyard vegetables making this dish easy and forgiving. So feel free to use any vegetables that are in season and/or easy to find.

Sturdier vegetables like broccoli, okra or mustard greens can go in with the fish. Delicate vegetables like *mizuna* and spinach can be added at the end.

If you'd like, serve the *sinigang* with a dipping sauce of fish sauce mixed with a squeeze of lemon or lime juice.

Steamed Fragrant Fish

Ever since I discovered how soft and silky fish turns out in the Instant Pot®, I've been hooked (no pun intended)! Please buy the freshest fish you can find, avoiding frozen fish if you can help it. Defrosted fish comes out too mushy when steamed.

PREP TIME: 10 minutes **TOTAL TIME:** 22 minutes
MAKES: 4 servings

2 tablespoons soy sauce
¼ teaspoon sesame oil
¼ teaspoon granulated sugar
3 tablespoons water
3 green onions, cut into thin, 3-inch (7.5-cm) strips, green and white parts separated (1 cup)
2-inch (5-cm) knob fresh ginger, peeled and cut into matchsticks (see Notes)
½ cup (25 g) cilantro/coriander leaves, roughly chopped
1 pound (450 g) fresh cod filets, or other firm white fish like tilapia or flounder, ¾ to 1 inch thick (2 to 2.5 cm)
2 tablespoons vegetable oil

SPECIAL EQUIPMENT
Steamer rack
7- to 8-inch (17.5- to 20-cm) heatproof container or rimmed plate (I use a 7-inch metal cake tin)
Parchment paper

1 Stir together the soy sauce, sesame oil, sugar and water in a small bowl.

2 Pour 1 cup water into the pot and nestle a steamer rack inside.

3 Line a heatproof container with parchment paper and arrange the fish in one layer. Cut the fish to fit if you have to. Scatter a few ginger shards on top. Place the container on the steamer rack.

4 Lock the lid. Select PRESSURE COOK/ MANUAL and set to LOW for 5 minutes. Make sure the steam release valve is sealed. Once pressurized (5 to 7 minutes), the cook cycle will start.

5 When the timer beeps, manually release the pressure. When the float valve drops, press CANCEL and open the lid.

6 Check the fish for doneness with a fork. If it flakes easily, it's done. If it's still opaque, cover the pot and cook the fish in the residual heat for another 1 to 2 minutes. Check every 30 seconds so you don't overcook the fish. Press CANCEL when done.

7 Wearing heatproof mitts, remove the fish and drain off the liquid. Grip the edges of the parchment paper and gently slide the fish onto a serving plate. Scatter the cilantro/coriander leaves and ⅓ of the green onions (only the green parts) over the steamed fish.

8 Heat the oil in a small saucepan over medium heat on the stove. Cook the remaining ginger until golden, about 1 minute. Add the rest of the green onions and the soy mixture. Stir and cook until the green onions wilt. Remove from the heat and pour over the fish. Serve immediately with steamed rice and a vegetable side dish.

> **NOTES:** Fresh ginger has stubborn fibers that run vertically along the entire rhizome and make it tough to chew. To get spicy, tender bites instead, slice the peeled ginger knob into thin slices lengthwise. The slices will be shaped like ovals or oblongs. Stack a few slices at a time and cut them lengthwise into fine, thin strips.

HOW TO PEEL AND SLICE GINGER

Desserts

Many Asian desserts are cooked in a steamer, making the Instant Pot® an excellent choice. Unlike steaming on the stovetop, a pressure cooker doesn't need a water refill, and there are no more burnt pots to clean!

Tapioca Pearls with Coconut Milk and Banana   Chè Chuối

Tapioca pearls are made from cassava root. I love them in this Vietnamese dessert (*che*) made with coconut milk and bananas.

PREP TIME: 5 minutes **TOTAL TIME:** 33 minutes
MAKES: 4 to 6 servings

½ cup (75 g) small tapioca pearls
1 (13½-ounce/400-ml) can coconut milk (or your favorite milk alternative)
½ cup (120 ml) water
½ cup (100g) sugar
⅛ teaspoon salt
1 *pandan* leaf, tied into a knot (optional)
3 ripe bananas, sliced into coins (save several slices for garnish)

SPECIAL EQUIPMENT
7- or 8-inch (17.5- to 20-cm) heatproof container (I use a 2-quart/2-l ceramic soufflé dish)
Steamer rack

1   Rinse the tapioca pearls in a fine-mesh strainer to remove excess starch. Drain over the sink while you prepare the rest of the ingredients.

2   Pour 1 cup (240 ml) water into the pot and nestle a steamer rack inside.

3   Mix together the tapioca pearls, coconut milk, water, sugar, *pandan* leaf and bananas in a heatproof container. Cover tightly with foil. Place the container on the rack.

4   Lock the lid. Select PRESSURE COOK/MANUAL and set to HIGH for 10 minutes. Make sure the steam release valve is sealed. Once pressurized (8 to 10 minutes), the cook cycle will start. When the timer beeps, let the pressure release naturally (about 10 minutes). When the float valve drops, press CANCEL and open the lid.

5   Lift the foil to check if the tapioca pearls are completely translucent with no white dot in their centers. If necessary, cook on HIGH PRESSURE for another 1 to 2 minutes. The second time around, quick release. When the float valve drops, press CANCEL and open the lid.

6   Wearing heatproof mitts, remove the tapioca and set it on a hot pad. Stir vigorously with a fork. Fish out the *pandan* leaf, if using. Spoon the tapioca into individual bowls or glasses. Garnish with extra sliced bananas before serving.

7   To serve cold, let cool before covering tightly with cling wrap. Refrigerate for at least 3 hours, or overnight.

> **NOTES:** If you prefer your pudding runny and porridgy rather than stiff and jiggly, simply increase the milk in this recipe by ½ cup (120 ml) or more.
> Instead of bananas, use 1 cup (175 g) sweet corn kernels.

Chocolate Rice Pudding — Champorado

While *champorado* is usually made with a glutinous rice called *malagkit*, I use short-grain Japanese sushi rice or arborio, depending on what I have in my pantry. In a pinch, you can even use jasmine or basmati rice.

PREP TIME: 5 minutes TOTAL TIME: 50 minutes
MAKES: 4 to 6 servings

1 cup (200 g) short-grain rice, rinsed and drained
2 cups (960 ml) whole milk (or any milk of your choice)
1¼ cups (300 ml) water
½ teaspoon ground cinnamon
Pinch of fine sea salt
1 teaspoon vanilla extract
⅓ to ½ cup (80 to 120 ml) sweetened condensed milk (depending on how sweet you like it), plus more for drizzling
1 (4-ounce/120-g) bar bittersweet chocolate, chopped, or ⅓ cup semi-sweet chocolate chips

1 Stir together the rice, milk, water, cinnamon and salt in the pot.
2 Lock the lid. Select PRESSURE COOK/MANUAL and set to HIGH for 20 minutes. Make sure the steam release valve is sealed. Once pressurized (12 to 15 minutes), the cook cycle will start.
3 When the timer beeps, let the pressure release naturally for 10 minutes. Then quick release any remaining pressure. When the float valve drops, press CANCEL and open the lid.

4 Wearing heatproof mitts, remove the inner pot and set it down on a hot pad. Add the vanilla, condensed milk and chocolate, and stir until the chocolate is melted and mixed into the rice.
5 Spoon the pudding into individual bowls, drizzle with more condensed milk and serve warm. Or cover and chill until cold and serve with fresh berries.

> **NOTE:** If you don't have sweetened condensed milk, use granulated sugar instead. Start with ¼ cup and adjust to taste.

Quick & Easy Flan

This Filipino-Style flan uses both evaporated and sweetened condensed milks. I've seen recipes that use up to 8 egg yolks, but I prefer moderation—I've only used 4 egg yolks and 2 whole eggs!

PREP TIME: 10 minutes **TOTAL TIME:** 1 hour, 10 minutes **MAKES:** 8 servings

Vegetable oil, for greasing
4 large egg yolks at room temperature
2 whole eggs at room temperature
1 (13½-ounce/400-ml) can sweetened condensed milk
1 (12-ounce/350-ml) can evaporated milk
1 teaspoon vanilla extract
Pinch fine sea salt
½ cup (200 g) granulated sugar
½ teaspoon lemon juice or white vinegar

SPECIAL EQUIPMENT
7- to 8-inch (17.5- to 20-cm) round cake pan (I use a 7-inch metal cake tin)
Steamer rack

1 Grease a round cake pan with vegetable oil. Pour 1 cup (240 ml) water into the pot and nestle a steamer rack inside.

2 Blitz the egg yolks, whole eggs, condensed milk, evaporated milk, vanilla and salt in a blender at low speed until very smooth. Or whisk in a mixing bowl. Set aside until needed.

3 Cook the sugar, lemon juice and 2 tablespoons water in a small saucepan on the stovetop over medium-low heat, stirring occasionally with a silicone spatula. Once the sugar begins to dissolve, about 5 minutes, stir constantly until it turns into a clear syrup. Stop stirring and raise the heat to medium. Swirl the saucepan every few minutes, until the caramel is dark golden brown, 8 to 10 minutes. Very carefully pour the caramel into the prepared cake pan. Wearing heatproof mitts, quickly tilt the pan to evenly coat the bottom and up the sides a bit. Place on the steamer rack in the pot.

4 Skim any foam off the surface of the custard and pour through a fine-mesh sieve into the caramel-lined cake pan. Cover tightly with foil.

5 Lock the lid. Select PRESSURE COOK/MANUAL and set to LOW for 10 minutes. Make sure the steam release valve is sealed. Once pressurized (7 to 10 minutes), the cook cycle will start.

6 When the timer beeps, let the pressure release naturally for 10 minutes. Then quick release any remaining pressure. When the float valve drops, press CANCEL and open the lid.

7 Wearing heatproof mitts, remove the flan and set it on a hot pad. The center of the flan will still be a little jiggly.

8 Let it cool for 30 minutes. Refrigerate for at least 6 hours before unmolding and serving.

9 To unmold, run a butter knife along the edges of the cake pan. Place a plate over the pan and flip it over quickly. Place the plate on a flat surface and let the flan loosen itself from the pan.

10 Cut into 8 wedges and serve with whipped cream and/or fresh fruit.

> **NOTES:** You can also serve the flan in small ramekins. Cook at LOW PRESSURE for 8 minutes before allowing the pressure to release naturally.

Chinese New Year Cake Nian Gao

Nian gao is usually served over the course of the 15 days of the Chinese (lunar) New Year celebrations when family and friends come to visit. To keep it fresh, wrap in plastic and refrigerate. When ready to serve, coat slices in egg and pan-fry. The result is a crisp outer shell and a soft chewy center.

PREP TIME: 10 minutes **TOTAL TIME:** 1 hour 5 minutes plus sitting time **MAKES:** One 7-inch (17.5-cm) cake

Vegetable oil, for greasing
1 cup (200 g) coconut sugar or ¾ cup (150 g) light brown sugar
1 cup (240 ml) water
2 cups (320 g) mochiko rice flour
Dried Chinese red dates, goji berries or toasted sesame seeds, for decoration

TO FINISH
Vegetable oil, for frying
1 to 2 large eggs (depending on how many slices you're frying), beaten until frothy

SPECIAL EQUIPMENT
7- to 8-inch (17.5- to 20-cm) ceramic or stainless-steel round cake pan (I use a 7-inch metal cake tin)
Steamer rack

1 Grease the cake pan with 1 teaspoon oil. (Or use 3 [5- to 6-inch/12.5- to 15-cm] ramekins). Line with parchment.
2 Dissolve the sugar in the water in a saucepan over medium heat. Remove from the heat and let cool about 10 minutes.
3 Sift the mochiko flour into the syrup, and stir with a silicon spatula until a smooth dough forms.
4 Turn the dough into the pan and pat down until it fills up the pan evenly. Lightly press a dried red date or 6 goji berries on top, or sprinkle with sesame seeds. Cover with foil.
5 Pour 1 cup (240 ml) water into the pot and nestle a steamer rack inside.
6 Lock the lid. Select PRESSURE COOK/MANUAL and set to HIGH for 30 minutes. Make sure the steam release valve is sealed. Once pressurized (8 to 10 minutes), the cook cycle will start. When the timer beeps, let the pressure release naturally

(about 15 minutes). When the float valve drops, press CANCEL and open the lid.
7 Remove the foil. The cake should be a deep caramel color and firm to the touch. Wearing heatproof mitts, remove the cake pan and set on a hot pad to cool. Cover loosely and leave at room temperature overnight.
8 The next day, run a knife along the edge of the cake to loosen it and invert onto a plate. Flip the cake right side up onto a cutting board and cut into quarters. Cut each quarter crosswise, not into wedges but into 2-inch-wide (5-cm) strips and cut each strip crosswise into scant ¼-inch-thick (6-mm) slices.
9 When ready to serve, coat a frying pan with oil and heat over medium until hot. Dip each slice into the egg and pan-fry in batches, cooking each side until golden-brown, about 2 to 3 minutes. Serve immediately.

NOTES: Mochiko is made from short-grain sweet rice and is gluten-free. It's used to make Japanese mochi and other confections as well as certain dim sum dishes. It's sold at many grocery stores, and most definitely at Asian markets. Other types of glutinous rice flour can be substituted.

Sweet Sticky Rice with Fresh Mango

The Instant Pot® makes preparing this dish very convenient because you don't have to soak the rice overnight. Be sure to buy glutinous rice, not Japanese-Style sushi/"sticky" rice. The texture is very different. If mangoes aren't in season, my recipe tester Kay suggests substituting bananas.

PREP TIME: 5 minutes TOTAL TIME: 30 minutes
MAKES: 4 to 6 servings

1 cup (200 g) glutinous rice (also called malagkit or sweet rice)
¾ cup (180 ml) water

COCONUT SAUCE
1 (13½-ounce/400-ml) can coconut milk, shaken
½ cup (100g) granulated sugar
½ teaspoon fine sea salt
1 pandan leaf tied into a knot (optional)
2 mangoes (about 6 oz/170 g each), peeled, pitted and sliced (see note)
Toasted sesame seeds, to garnish

SPECIAL EQUIPMENT
7- to 8-inch (17.5- to 20-cm) bowl or round cake pan (I use a 7-inch metal cake tin)
Steamer rack

1 Rinse the rice and drain in a fine-mesh sieve over the sink.
2 Pour 1 cup (240 ml) water into the pot and nestle a steamer rack inside.
3 Tip the drained rice into a bowl and place it on the steamer rack. Pour in ¾ cup (180 ml) cold water over the rice and smooth down to submerge.
4 Lock the lid. Select PRESSURE COOK/MANUAL and set to HIGH for 12 minutes. Make sure the steam release valve is sealed. Once pressurized (8 to 10 minutes), the cook cycle will start.
5 Meanwhile, make the coconut sauce. Simmer the coconut milk with the pandan leaf (if using) in a small saucepan over medium heat. Stir frequently and watch that it doesn't start to boil. Whisk in the sugar and salt until dissolved and take off the heat.

Remove the pandan leaf and taste. The coconut sauce should taste salty-sweet.
6 When the timer beeps, let the pressure release naturally for 10 minutes. Then quick release any remaining pressure. When the float valve drops, press CANCEL and open the lid.
7 Wearing heatproof mitts, transfer the cooked rice to a large heatproof bowl. Fold in half the coconut sauce and let the rice absorb all the liquid, about 20 minutes (or leave for up to 2 hours at room temperature.)
8 When ready to serve, mound the coconut rice onto small plates and arrange the mango on top or alongside. Drizzle the rice with more sauce and garnish with toasted sesame seeds. Serve immediately.

> NOTES: Using a stainless-steel container is ideal, but if you use a ceramic bowl, increase the cooking time by 5 minutes.
> Pandan leaves are available frozen (sometimes fresh) at Asian markets and are considered the vanilla of Southeast Asia. Substitute 1 teaspoon vanilla extract if you can't find it, or just omit.

HOW TO CUT A MANGO

You can use this hedgehog method to cut the mangoes. Slice each mango down either side of the stone.
   Score lines across and down the mango flesh in a crisscross pattern at 1-inch (2.5-cm) intervals, stopping at the skin. Turn the skin inside out so the mango pieces pop up. Slice the mango flesh as close to the skin as possible and cubes will come off. Trim the skin off the middle bit where the stone is, then cut them into cubes as well so you are not throwing any extra flesh away.

HOW TO MAKE THE COCONUT RICE

Index

Published by Tuttle Publishing, an imprint of Periplus Editions (HK) Ltd.

www.tuttlepublishing.com

Text © 2020 Patricia Tanumihardja
Photographs © 2020 Sarah Culver except for those listed under Photo Credits

Library of Congress Cataloging-in-Publication Data in Process

Isbn: 978-0-8048-5257-9

DISTRIBUTED BY
North America, Latin America & Europe
Tuttle Publishing
364 Innovation Drive
North Clarendon, VT 05759-9436 U.S.A.
Tel: 1 (802) 773-8930; Fax: 1 (802) 773-6993
info@tuttlepublishing.com
www.tuttlepublishing.com

Japan
Tuttle Publishing
Yaekari Building 3rd Floor
5-4-12 Osaki Shinagawa-ku, Tokyo 141-0032
Tel: (81) 3 5437-0171; Fax: (81) 3 5437-0755
sales@tuttle.co.jp
www.tuttle.co.jp

Asia Pacific
Berkeley Books Pte. Ltd.
3 Kallang Sector #04-01
Singapore 349278
Tel: (65) 6741 2178; Fax: (65) 6741 2179
inquiries@periplus.com.sg
www.tuttlepublishing.com

23 22 21   10 9 8 7 6 5 4 3 2

Printed in Singapore   2103TP

"Books to Span the East and West"

Tuttle Publishing was founded in 1832 in the small New England town of Rutland, Vermont [USA]. Our core values remain as strong today as they were then—to publish best-in-class books which bring people together one page at a time. In 1948, we established a publishing office in Japan—and Tuttle is now a leader in publishing English-language books about the arts, languages and cultures of Asia. The world has become a much smaller place today and Asia's economic and cultural influence has grown. Yet the need for meaningful dialogue and information about this diverse region has never been greater. Over the past seven decades, Tuttle has published thousands of books on subjects ranging from martial arts and paper crafts to language learning and literature—and our talented authors, illustrators, designers and photographers have won many prestigious awards. We welcome you to explore the wealth of information available on Asia at**www.tuttlepublishing.com**.

Limit of Liability/Disclaimer of Warranty

The Publisher and the author make no representations or warranties with respect to the accuracy or completeness of the contents of this work and specifically disclaim all warranties, including without limitation warranties of fitness for a particular purpose. No warranty may be created or extended by sales or promotional materials. The advice and strategies contained herein may not be suitable for every situation. This work is sold with the understanding that the Publisher is not engaged in rendering medical, legal or other professional advice or services. If professional assistance is required, the services of a competent professional person should be sought. Neither the Publisher nor the author shall be liable for damages arising herefrom.

Acknowledgment

This book wouldn't have been possible without the help and support of so many people! I'd like to thank the staff at Tuttle Publishing, especially my editor Doug Sanders. I couldn't have done it without my team of recipe testers: Marcie Flinchum Atkins, Angelica Avila, Jeanne Bulla, Naomi Capili, Elizabeth Tveit Flajole, Emily Hilderman, Patricia Holm, Grace Hwang Lynch Laura McCarthy, Elizabeth Ann Quirino, Kayleen Takase, Lenny Teh, Aleena Wee. And of course I'm indebted to my personal recipe tasters—my husband, Omar, and son, Isaac.

Photo Credits

Periplus Editions (HK) Ltd *page 19;* istockphoto.com/SweetBabeeJay *page 70;* istockphoto.com/Richard Ernest Yap *page 71*
Following stock photos from **Shutterstock.com**
adrian agulto *page 82;* Atsushi Hirao *page 47;* **bonchan** *inside back cover; pages 62; 94; 123;* BorisKotov *page 61;* comzeal images *back cover; page 113;* DesignStory99 *page 24;* Ezume Images *back cover; page 40;* Foodio *page 112;* Gaak *cover spine; page 2;* **gowithstock** *back cover; inside front cover; pages 86; 98; 101; 102;* homelesscuisine *page 39;* IJAEVECTORTHAI *page 32;* Indian Food Images *page 42;* jantenthousand *page 29;* **Jaromir Klein** *page 34;* jejim *page 115;* Joshua Resnick *page 3;* jreika *page 80;* Junjira Konsang *page 118;* karins *inside back cover;* Kidsada Manchinda *inside front cover; page 66;* **Kiian Oksana** *page 2;* Lesya Dolyuk *pages 5; 78; 84;* Lukas Gojda *front cover;* **Ms.Giggles** *page 104;* mokokomo *page 93;* monofaction *page 33;* Natalia Livingston *front cover; page 103;* **Nataliya Arzamasova** *page 121;* nelea33 *page 122;* nesavinov *page 43;* norikko *page 31;* oumjeab *page 120;* papi8888 *page 110;* Paul_Brighton *page 105;* Piyato *back cover; pages 73; 107;* Ravsky *page 41;* Samart Mektippachai *page 52;* sasaken *page 28;* Sentelia *page 51;* SharkPaeCNX *inside front cover; pages 9; 56;* shigemi okano *page 77;* Siim79 *inside back cover; pages 6; 22;* successo images *front cover; pages 44; 68;* Tataya Kudo *page 23;* Tatiana Volgutova *back cover; page 90;* Timolina *page 99;* TMON *page 81;* vm2002 *front cover; pages 45; 49; 69;* Urvashi-A *page 30;* Wisnu Yudowibowo *inside back cover; page 97;* woeiwoeiwoei *page 65*